THE UNFAIR ADVANTAGE

Sell With NLP!

Revised Edition

By Duane Lakin, Ph.D.

D r. Duane Lakin is a psychologist and business consultant. A graduate of the University of Minnesota, Duane has over thirty years of experience serving business leaders as an industrial psychologist. Prior to that, he was a clinical psychologist and school consultant.

Since the mid-1980's, he has been looking at ways to make NLP (neurolinguistic programming) useful to sales people. Sales representatives have told him clearly that they are not interested in touchy-feely theories or complex analytical approaches to selling. Having worked for three decades in the business arena as a contributor to the hiring process for sales people, managers, and executives, he has seen ample proof that selling is hard enough without making it more difficult. At the same time, he has discovered that few sales people are trained in how to sell themselves and how to use language to increase their effectiveness.

His workshop, The Unfair Advantage—Sell with NLP!, has been presented to representatives of over 750 companies in the U.S., U.K., Russia, Hungary, Italy, and Canada. His research and consulting in NLP applications to telemarketing are unique in the industry. He has trained managers from companies such as Xerox, PacBell, Andersen Consulting, American General, Cable and Wireless, Hewlett Packard, GE, and many others. He has written or contributed to articles in Selling Power, HR Magazine, Production and Inventory Management, and Sales and Marketing Excellence. He has also talked to many professional organizations on NLP as well as interviewing skills. He is a recipient of the "TEC 200" and "Vistage 100 Achievement Award" designations for outstanding resource speakers to TEC (now called Vistage). He is also a member of the National Speakers Association.

This book, based on the workshop, is consistently the top rated book on NLP for sales. You can read the reviews at Amazon.com. It has been translated and published in Romanian, Polish and Spanish languages. An audio version of the original edition of the book is available as is a video of a live workshop.

Dr. Lakin's new series of ten online (on-demand) advanced lessons can now be seen at www.SellWithNLP.com. Each lesson covers the skills needed to be more effective in each stage of a typical selling cycle from how to get invited to meet with a prospect to handling objections or matching a proposal to a client. The first lesson can be viewed at no charge. He has also launched a new series called "The Ten-Minute Advantage" that introduces one skill at a time in a short ten-minute on-line lesson.

Lakin Associates
25W484 Flint Creek Road
Wheaton, IL 60189-7373
630-871-2996
www.SellWithNLP.com

• Public Workshops
• Customized In-House Workshops
• "On-Line" Workshop

This publication is the property of Lakin Associates and protected under the copyright laws in effect in 2012. It contains ideas and information that are considered to be of proprietary nature and interest to Lakin Associates. No reproduction or redistribution of the ideas and descriptions contained herein are authorized. No part of this book may be reproduced or transmitted in any form or by any means, electronic or mechanical, including photocopying, recording, or by any information storage and retrieval system without permission in writing from the author.

ISBN 978-0-9679162- 4-8 (Revised Edition)

www.SellWithNLP.com

PREFACE to REVISED EDITION

The _Unfair Advantage: Sell with NLP!_ is **not** a book about NLP. It is a book for sales people who want to have an advantage in everything that they say, write and do.

This book is for sellers. It is for people who want to find an edge--an advantage in the field. Much of The Unfair Advantage: Sell with NLP! is based on NLP skills, which is why NLP is in the title. But NLP is much more and much less than what is seen in this book. The techniques and skills here have been fine-tuned by me for the last 30 years for only one purpose: to help sales professionals be more effective and successful.

All selling is personal. People do not buy from companies. People want to talk to people they trust. People buy from people. The person who can sell himself or herself most effectively has a distinct advantage. The Unfair Advantage: Sell with NLP! teaches you how to be more effective in selling YOU and controlling the selling process.

The Revised Edition has two new chapters: Handling Objections Without Losing Rapport and Mindsets (Metaprograms). There has also been some minor tweaking and an attempt to catch typing errors in the previous edition while making new ones in this one. The Revised Edition has also been reformatted to allow it to be printed as an e-book and to be sold for a lesser price. In this way, I hope to expand the audience and give more people an advantage.

I hope you find the Revised Edition helpful. If you already own the original book, unless you specifically want the e-book format, I would not recommend that you buy the Revised Edition. Instead, contact me, and I will send you the two new chapters.

Good reading and enjoy the advantage.

Duane Lakin, Ph.D.
Wheaton, IL
drlakin@SellWithNLP.com
www.SellWithNLP.com

PREFACE

"It goes likes this. Let's see now: 'Protect me from knowing what I don't need to know. Protect me from even knowing that there are things to know that I don't know. Protect me from knowing that I decided not to know about the things that I decided not to know about. Amen.' That's it.

"There's another prayer that goes with it...It goes, 'Lord, Lord, Lord...Protect me from the consequences of the above prayer. Amen." —from <u>Mostly Harmless</u> by Douglas Adams

"The human mind treats a new idea the same way the body treats a strange protein—it rejects it." —P. B. Medawar

"*But this isn't what they taught us in marketing!*" This was the cry of a participant in a recent The Unfair Advantage® workshop. She was having to come to grips with the fact that the world continues to change, and she must change her view of how to sell to that moving target. And so must you.

You are entering the era of the *market niche of one*. Instead of trying to focus on a broad marketplace, you must know how to sell to a specific individual, one who may be talking to you right now in Chicago or reading your ad in Poughkeepsie or Winnipeg. You must be prepared to respond to what is unique about every individual you meet every time you get an opportunity. "Tried-and-true" approaches that rely on rigid scripts or general marketing assumptions about customers are not flexible or powerful enough today to get the results you want. If you want the "unfair advantage," you must learn to gather new information and use that information effectively.

Now more than ever, the customer has enormous control. The customer has access to more information than can possibly be processed. You must compete with all other possible activities and interests of the customer, not just with similar products or services. When someone can watch any of 500 television channels on a 24-hour basis, read instant news or stock reports from a computer screen, choose which ad to watch on television or which player on the football field the camera will follow during a game, or turn to a home shopping network and buy next week's wardrobe, the concept of selling must change. The message you send to differentiate your product or to make you stand out as a sales person must be personal, flexible, inviting, and designed for one rather than for many. More than ever, you must sell YOU, and the message must get through the clutter and noise of all the other messages in the air.

The "Unfair Advantage" is the ability to sell YOU.

This book is the result of twenty years of practicing and teaching some basic principles of persuasive communication. During my career, the techniques I used to accomplish my goals were called several names, depending on what I was doing at the time:

- *teaching*
- *training*
- *psychotherapy*
- *consulting*
- *selling*
- *marketing*
- *advertising*

These different names or different types of communication all share several characteristics:

1. *They are all persuasive skills.* That is, they are all used to influence how someone thinks or acts. Even as a consultant, my objective is to get someone to **do** something new rather than just convey information. (This book is written to make you want to act in a new more effective way, for instance.)

2. *They all work.* The techniques get results. As a psychotherapist, I was doing successful behavior-based "short-term therapy" before managed-care organizations started mandating such approaches. As a teacher and trainer, I teach people how to create change in others, and as an independent consultant, I help people make useful decisions. I also sell my services. I often warn people who invite me to visit to discuss The Unfair Advantage for their companies, "I practice what I teach."

3. *They all use the same set of techniques to be successful!* The communication techniques needed to be successful in directing therapy differ little from those needed to sell or teach. A behavioral analysis of successful sales professionals, successful therapists, or inspiring teachers yields the same set of communication techniques. Successful persuasion uses communication skills that are common to all settings. This is why my clients include service industries, law firms, manufacturing companies, and even a church seminary.

4. *Anyone can learn The Unfair Advantage.* I have introduced these ideas and techniques to over 500 CEOs in the U.S., U.K., and Canada in addition to hundreds of other professionals in sales and management. They have used the skills to improve their impact on their subordinates, to develop better marketing materials, and to provide power to their selling efforts, such as two reported cases where two different workshop participants used some of the techniques to close specific deals worth over $5 million each.

In the early 1970's, a name was given to these techniques—*Neurolinguistic Programming.* Although an argument can easily be made for the need to find a better name, it is descriptive: Our neurology affects how we think (*neuro*), and therefore, how we speak (*linguistic*). Also, how we speak reveals how we think. By understanding how to apply those principles, you can become a persuasive communicator, one who can make others think and act, whether they want to or not (*programming*).

As you decide how to use the ideas in this workbook, read it first for fun and then for profit, because you will discover in these pages the power of speaking and writing for impact.

The Unfair Advantage can be learned by anyone who may want to learn something new, even though old ways of doing things seem easier or at least more familiar. While it may be said, "The best way is the way you know," the successful professional is the person who decides to learn a new way.

I was walking with a woman in downtown Chicago one morning. I noticed as we would approach a grating in the sidewalk, she would move to the edge of the street to avoid walking on it. This maneuver was not easy, since the sidewalks were crowded with commuters. She would have to weave between people each time she made her lateral move, like a running back heading for the sideline. It was slowing her progress and causing her to work much harder than would seem necessary to maneuver through the normal clutter of the city.

After watching her do this several times, I finally asked her why. She replied, "Oh, I learned to do this years ago when I first started working downtown. I ruined so many pairs of high-heels. The grates catch the heel of my shoes and break them, so I learned to stay on the edge of the sidewalk. It's second nature to me now."

"But", I said, "You are wearing tennis shoes!"

I am not a theorist. I am an engineer. A behavioral engineer. I am interested in things that work, things that help me help others create change. The Unfair Advantage works, and it can work for you. To paraphrase a routine from Saturday Night Live, "**Read it now, believe it later.**"

TABLE of CONTENTS

Chapter 1: What is NLP? 1

Chapter 2: NLP and Selling 9

Chapter 3: The "Engineered" Selling Process 23

Chapter 4: Language of the Mind 30

Chapter 5: Language Pacing 45

Chapter 6: Addressing a VAK-Mixed Audience 72

Chapter 7: Using Eye Cues...86

Chapter 8: Buying Patterns 103

Chapter 9: Non-Verbal Mirroring 112

Chapter 10: Creating Action With Words 122

Chapter 11: Embedding the Action Command....................140

Chapter 12: Mindsets (Metaprograms)..............................159

Chapter 13: Handling Objections Without Losing Rapport....212

Chapter 14: Keeping the Advantage 223

Chapter 15: Special Application: Presentations/Team Selling...233

Chapter 16: Special Application: Letters/Memo Writing 238

Chapter 17: Special Application: Telemarketing 243

Addendum A-1

    A. Follow-Up Checklist of Techniques

    B. Language Preference Indicator (LPI)

    C. Workshop Outline

1 *What is NLP?*

When Pericles spoke, people said, "How well he speaks,"
but when Demosthenes spoke, they said, "Let us march."
—from Paul LeRoux in <u>Selling to A Group: Presenta-</u>
<u>tion Strategies</u>

INTRODUCTION

Your job is to influence people. You use all the skills you
have. But as you know, some days it works and some
days it does not. You can be hot one day and ice cold
the next. There are days you can talk until you turn blue and
nothing happens. Sometimes words just fail to get the results
you want to see. And then there are the days when you can say
no wrong and everything seems to work.

On the good days, people are often eager to take credit for
their success, but those same people prefer to blame the audience for the bad days:

"The customer was resistant."
"They weren't ready to buy today."
"The price was too high."
"The competition killed us."
"Kids—they never listen."

1

But the problem is not the audience...it is you!

Yet, you are the same person on the good days as on the bad ones. In many cases, you are selling the same product or service, and you may be preaching the same message to the same people on both days.

So why do you see different results?

The answer is found in your words and how you use them.

COMMUNICATION FAILURES

I have spent nearly twenty-five years helping people communicate better. Whether I was helping a struggling salesman or talking with a manager who needed to be a better coach to her assistant, I have been involved in communication problems in hundreds of different forms. As I traveled this journey, I discovered two reasons that account for most failed communication.

• Failure to Notice

First, people who are *not* effective communicators often do not notice they are having a problem.

Have you ever heard a sales representative say *"Wow, we have this deal locked up. They loved us!"* only to discover the next day that someone else got the business? Or perhaps you have seen the engineer who says, *"I know exactly what the customer wants and here it is"* only to find much later that the product is not what the customer wants at all. Maybe you have watched someone trying to make their point long after the audience was no longer listening. These are all examples of people not knowing they did not communicate. Unlike the popular movie, there was no one shouting, *"What we have here is a failure to communicate!"*

2

Sometimes people fail to notice simply because they are **too focused on themselves**. If you are worrying about how you look or sound, you will not notice your impact on others.

Another reason people seem to fail to notice that they are not being effective is a **lack of options**. Without options, they may lack the courage to notice that they are not being effective. If you are trying to sell something and you have given your best pitch, you cannot afford to notice that you have not been successful. If you *do* see your lack of impact or feel that things are not going well, what are you going to say next? You have already given your best and you have nothing better to offer!

A lack of response options is the single biggest reason for people to ignore the cues that tell you when you are not being effective. Without options, you cannot respond. You do not know where to go next. Therefore, you simply choose not to notice. Noticing failure takes courage, but it also requires that you have a Plan B available. Most people lack this advantage.

• Failure to Repeat

The second discovery about communication I have noticed is that most people who *are* effective communicators fail to know why. As a result, they cannot be consistently effective.

Remember when you had a great day—when everything went well and you sold your ideas effectively? The next morning, you are energized and ready to see another successful day. However, this day does not go so well. People are not listening. Your ideas are being challenged. No one is buying. What happened? It's not so different from being able to hit a drive 280 yards on the practice tee, straight and down the middle of the fairway, and then finding it impossible to miss a single sand trap on the rest of the course. If you do not know what you did right, you cannot do it again.

Most successful sales and management professionals do not know what they do that makes them successful. They are what is often called "unconscious competents." As a result, when things are going well, they have difficulty knowing why. When something works well one day, they cannot repeat it the next time. It also means they cannot teach their skills to others. *Have you ever seen a top sales representative promoted to sales manager only to discover he cannot teach what he knows?*

Not knowing why you are successful one day means you may not be able to repeat your success when you need it. Without such insight, whether you are selling a product, directing a work group or writing advertising copy, success on Tuesday does not increase the chances of success on Wednesday.

In short, the reason for most communication failures can be summarized as follows:

1. If there is a problem, you ignore the cues, either because you do not notice or because you do not know what else to do.

2. If there is no *problem, you do not know what you did right and cannot repeat it.*

NLP: THE PIECES OF THE PUZZLE

In the early 1970's, I was involved in the new and evolving psychology of family therapy. In studying the work of therapists and theorists like Virginia Satir, Paul Watslawik, Gregory Bateson, Milton Erickson, Carl Whitaker, and others, my colleagues and I were exploring new territory that had few established rules and emphasized observable results. One outcome of this new perspective on therapy and change was the recognition that some people had skills that consistently changed people's attitudes and behaviors while the rest of us struggled to have consistent impact.

At one point, I was trying to teach a young intern how to work more effectively as a family therapist and was having little success. I was certain my lack of success was due to his resistant and unresponsive manner rather than my clumsy teaching. One day he returned from a workshop in California, and said to me *"I just took a course called Neurolinguistic Programming. And it was amazing. They were teaching the same things you are trying to teach me. But when they did it, it made sense!"* Thus began my journey into NLP.

NLP—or Neurolinguistic Programming[1]—is based on the observations of John Grinder and Richard Bandler. Trying to answer why some people were effective as change agents and others were not, they began to label the *patterns* of language and communication that led to successful influence and persuasion. They watched and listened to many people until they were able to distinguish the patterns that led to *consistent* success. They then modeled these patterns themselves and discovered that by following the same linguistic and non-verbal patterns of communication, they could create change too! As they expanded their study and categorized their observations, their taxonomy of interactional patterns became known as NLP.

NLP identified and labeled the patterns of communication that created successful change in others. Whether we were sales professionals or therapists, we now knew *what to notice*. We could teach ourselves and others to be more observant and responsive. In addition, we now had different response patterns from which to choose. We had *choices for responding* to others and to different situations. We had a Plan A, B, or C, depending on what was needed.

Since 1970, NLP has grown from a relatively unknown set of techniques for therapists to a multi-million dollar self-help industry due to the efforts of Anthony Robbins and others. Like any good idea, NLP has been thoughtfully applied in some arenas as well as foolishly promoted or misrepresented in others. But the fundamental observations and discoveries remain sound. Patterns of communication that influence people and can create change have been labeled and replicated, and these patterns can be used by anyone in the business of selling or persuading.

PRINCIPLES OF NLP

Several principles may help you understand the link between words, psychology, and persuasion that helps account for the power of NLP skills.

1. We perceive information quickly without awareness.

The nonconscious[2] mind can receive information and even make decisions. In fact, the mind reacts more quickly to nonconscious stimuli than it does when the conscious mind is aware of what is being seen or heard. The conscious mind seems to add resistance and context confusion. The message is slowed, filtered and even distorted at times. Much of what we call "intuition" is really perception outside our conscious awareness.

2. We can influence our nonconscious mind.

Much of what we do is nonconscious. We breathe, we cough, we yawn. We do not usually think, *"Gee, I guess I will take a breath now."* Yet something as automatic as our heartbeat can be influenced by our thinking.

> *Try this: Tell yourself to feel your heart, listen to the beat. Now tell yourself to speed up your heart rate.*

Take a deep breath. Now redirect your attention to your left hand. Tell yourself to think about your left hand tingling. Notice the effect?

Our ability to control the autonomic nervous system is the basis of what is now called biofeedback. We can train our nervous system. We can, therefore, train our thinking, because thinking is a nervous system or neurological activity. That is, we can *program* our minds to work for us through self-talk, which is what *thinking* really is. Therefore, *neurolinguistic programming* refers to the ability of our mind to influence behavior as well as the fact that our behavior reveals how our mind is working. This interrelationship is the basis for self-help training such as visualization, self-affirmation or the power of positive thinking.

3. We can influence the nonconscious thinking of others.

Language is the pathway to the nonconscious mind[3]. Words create brain activity. By using words effectively, we can bypass conscious resistance and create mental activity, not just in our minds but in the thinking processes of others. (Why else would this be a book for sales and management professionals?)

For instance, read this sentence: *Do not think of a pink elephant!*

Thinking about that pink elephant, are you? Yet the message said "Do **not** think of a pink elephant." So why are you still seeing that elephant in your mind?

Because the words could not be ignored! The mind responded even though the actual words said "*Do not...*" (This phenomena will be explained later in Chapter 11.)

Communication patterns that can carry a message without being noticed or resisted will be more effective than those that must compete with conscious resistance and filtering. The brain must react, even if the conscious mind is unaware.

4. Mental activity precedes (and often directs) behavior.

A mental *decision* to act occurs before the *behavior* occurs and even before a conscious decision is clarified. In practical terms, this means that a person's decision to buy or to believe often happens BEFORE he or she is aware of making that decision. No wonder people often invent such wonderful rationalizations for things they do! The real reasons are often nonconscious. By influencing mental activity, we can influence the behavior that follows. *"People sometimes consciously plan and then act, but more often behavior is influenced by unconscious processes; that is, people act and then, if called upon, make excuses."*[4]

NLP has identified a set of techniques that can consistently influence our thinking and the thinking of others. With NLP, you can create mental activity AND get behavior change in subtle yet effective ways. When used in a context of integrity and professionalism, it is powerful and productive. With a little effort and the courage to try something different, you can learn NLP techniques and have The Unfair Advantage.

[1]Neurolinguistic Programming was originally coined by Alfred Korzybski. It refers to the interrelationship of the mind and language. The way we think influences or *programs* the way we use language. Similarly, the way we speak reveals our thinking process.

[2]The word "nonconsciously" is used to avoid the historical differentiation in psychology between "unconscious" and "subconscious." "Nonconscious" simply means that the conscious mind is not aware of the stimulus. Sometimes this is referred to as "subliminal."

[3]from Patterns in the Mind, Jackendoff, Ray, Basic Books, 1994.

[4]from *Unconscious influences revealed*, Jacoby, Larry L., D. Stephen Lindsay, and Jeffrey P. Toth, in *American Psychologist*, June 1992, Volume 47, No. 6, 802-809.

2 *NLP and Selling*

"If people around you will not hear you, fall down before them and beg their forgiveness, for in truth you are to blame." —Fyodor Dostoyevsky

INTRODUCTION

Not all words are created equal. Some sell. Some inform. Some do nothing at all. Read the following note: *"Dear customer: We have initiated a series of procedures to dialogue with our facilitators, to coordinate various strategies that impact the process in terms of the dynamics involved in the partnering between our businesses and the functionality of our services..."*

Yecch! Such drivel puts anyone to sleep. Yet, somewhere in the lives of most business professionals, there must have been a lecture on "How to write and sound professional." Or more honestly, "How to write and be boring." It could also have been titled "How to influence nobody." Too often, your attempt to sound "business-like" kills the chances of your message being heard.

Why should someone buy from you? What is the difference between your ad and the thousand other commercial messages an individual hears in a single day? Will anyone remember your memo? Is your solicitation looked at as junk mail or as welcome information? Did your voice-mail message get a response? Did your telephone sales message work? Do people remember that you left a message?

If you have something to say, you should be willing to package that message to give it power.

CONTENT DOES NOT SELL ITSELF

A well-delivered message will:
- Be heard by more people with fewer words
- Sell a vision, not just a product, service, or idea
- Carry a message faster and more convincingly
- Build and maintain rapport

It is not what we say that makes a difference. It is how we say it and how it is received. Words create action but only if they are engineered to do so.

There seems to be a myth held by many people that a strong message or a great idea will sell itself.

How foolish!

If an idea could sell itself, every great idea would be embraced and only the best proposals would ever be accepted. No sales person would ever worry about seeing a resistant customer again.

If you are a manager, people who work for you do not respond to your ideas simply because your ideas are so profound or brilliant. If you write advertisements, you know that clever or informative copy does not ensure sales. If you are a seller of goods or services, you know customers do not buy your product or proposal simply because you tell them to do so. A better mousetrap, or a better idea, will not be sufficient to drive customers to your door.

SELLING IS DIFFERENT THAN TELLING

Telling conveys information. Selling leads to an action.

Telling focuses on the sender. Selling focuses on the receiver.

Telling does not get results. If it does not work with your kids, it will not work with your customers.

Why would you ever want to settle for simply *telling* when you can also create action?

What you do in management, sales or marketing is to use language to accomplish your goal: appointments, meetings, hirings and firings, persuading and negotiating. All of these activities are intended to persuade people, to get a result. Rarely do you communicate that you are not trying to persuade or sell. You may be clarifying goals, setting plans, evaluating for performance enhancement, or trying to convince others of the merit of your idea. Language is about the constitution of action rather than sounds. [1]

Results require selling, not telling.

It is your use of words that can give you the Unfair Advantage as a sales or marketing professional, a manager, or simply someone who wants to be persuasive.

If you use words the right way, you can create the action you want. Failure to understand this important fact leads to millions of wasted advertising dollars and millions more dollars wasted in ineffective sales activities. Clever ads and persistent sales professionals may impress management, but they are often inefficient approaches to persuasion and selling. To paraphrase a familiar comment, *sell the mind and the individual will follow.*

In recent research with an international telemarketing firm, I had the opportunity to really prove the power of "Message Engineering™." By simply changing the wording of a telephone script, we achieved sales increases of 16%, 30%, and 35% in three different campaigns!

11

When you carefully engineer words, you can have a distinct and measurable advantage. If you ignore the importance of an engineered message, your words will fail to sell.

WHY DO WORDS OFTEN FAIL TO PERSUADE?

There are several roadblocks that keep you from selling as effectively as you would like.

1. The message is not noticed.

People are bombarded by words and messages. Television, radio, newspapers, mail, and normal conversation all compete for attention. This creates noise which prevents the message from being heard.

> *Listen for a moment to the sounds around you. Pick one to notice. Does it seem to get louder? Now pick a different sound. Now the new sound becomes dominant. The sounds have not changed, but your ability to hear one or another sound has altered.*

The mind cannot handle all the sensory information available to it. If we were unable to sort and filter information, we could not function in a normal manner. Consider the behavior of hyperactive or autistic children. These are people who cannot effectively process the information their senses gather. As a result, they do not function normally as they try to manage the confusion that is their experience of the world. We need our mind to filter information to enable us to manage the quantity of "noise" that is around us every day or we would all suffer from sensory overload.

We also filter information by our biases. We see what we want to see. We resist what we do not want to hear. George Johnson writes in <u>In the Palaces of Memory</u>, "Minds are not mirrors; they are interpreting all the time."[2] Through generalization, deletion or reduction of information, and other forms of conscious and unconscious filtering, we allow only certain information to pass to our conscious mind. When we are alert to certain information, such as when we have a clearly defined personal goal in mind, this focus on an outcome helps us receive relevant information through our sensory filter. Consequently, we suddenly see or hear useful ideas or opportunities that help us achieve our goal. Without sensitivity to relevant information, potentially useful information goes unnoticed. [3]

2. The message does not fit the audience.

People hear and notice what is familiar to them. Words and phrases that look or feel familiar will have more of an impact on people than the unfamiliar. A philosophy professor addressing a group of industrial engineers will have difficulty speaking their language. Ideas may be expressed, but concepts will not be embraced by the audience. Too often, people talk or write the way that makes *them* feel comfortable and ignore what is necessary to make the audience feel good or be open to the message.

> *A creative team created a successful television ad for Apple Computer titled "1984". It was aired during the 1984 Super Bowl. It was a huge success. The same team was given another contract for the 1985 Super Bowl. They created another ad that was equally unusual and visually creative. The team liked it a lot even though the people at Apple were not fond of it. Nevertheless, it aired. The result? The new ad bombed. The audience apparently hated it, too.[4]*

In many marketing departments, product managers decide what to do on the basis of "What do I like?" rather than "What fits my customer?" I once interviewed a young product manager with the Quaker Oats Company who told me he was allocating tens of thousands of dollars on a campaign for one of their consumer products based on the fact that *"I like this approach better. It works for me."* This logic is typical of many sales and marketing professionals. They fail to recognize that there is no advantage when the emphasis is on *your* likes and attitudes instead of trying to fit the delivery of your message to your audience.

3. The message does not include an action.

Some messages are not intended to sell. They are meant to convey information or create an image. Look at the advertisements in your favorite magazine or newspaper. How many have action statements, such as "buy" or "get our product?" Often, advertisers are seeking name recognition rather than trying to sell the reader or listener. Yet, it seems wasteful to spend money on a message that could be selling as well as creating an image.

RULES OF THE UNFAIR ADVANTAGE

To gain and hold an advantage in sales, you need to understand the psychological rules that govern buying and selling. People buy in a predictable way. Once you recognize and adapt to this set of rules, you are on your way to gaining the advantage.

1. Rapport precedes a sale.

People will only buy from someone they trust. Rapport must come first. People decide to buy the person before they buy the service or idea. You "buy" me; then you evaluate what I am selling. As long as I am selling something that meets a need for you, I have the sale. Once you have sold yourself, the actual sale is only yours to lose. Without rapport, the sale is nearly impossible.

2. People buy for their own reasons and in their own way.

Sales training typically focuses on features and benefits. This is a useful approach. A good sales person needs to know what a product or service *may* provide a customer.

But when it is time to sell, the key is learning how to adapt to what the customer wants, not learning how to recite the benefits that the service provider or manufacturer believe are important.

> *For decades, IBM was proud of its training programs. It taught young professionals how to present features and highlight the benefits of IBM's products. Trainees would rehearse in front of their peers until they got it right. But they often failed to learn to listen to the customer. The IBM sales professionals were excellent presenters and knew the product, but they failed to sell to the individual customer. They sold the way mass marketing works—they were trying to get their message to the widest audience. As a result, the market changed and left them in trouble. They knew their product. They did not hear their customer.*

3. The Golden Rule is Wrong!

At least in the sales arena it is. The effective communicator understands that you do *not* "do unto others as you would want them to do unto you." The Golden Rule is great advice for friends and neighbors, and it promotes civilized behavior. But it does not create change or persuade others.

> *A young man I know in California is determined to be a successful salesman. He is selling a service to medical offices and industrial plants. He starts each day the same way—he enters a large multi-office building, goes to the top floor, and begins to knock on every door until he reaches the first floor. He is proud of his persistence and tenacity. He approaches every prospect with the same opening comments, and he leaves his business card as he exits. He makes over 100 calls before he generates a qualified lead.*

This young man is not selling. He is taking his sales approach door-to-door, hoping someone will buy it. He likes his style, and he hopes others will like it, too. This sales style works only if you live long enough to find people who will put up with you— people who want to be sold the way you want to sell.

Selling, whether it is selling a product, a service, or an idea, requires flexibility. Doing the same thing over and over is good for practicing a golf swing but poor salesmanship. Once the game has begun, the successful sales professional, like the low-handicap golfer, plays the ball as it lies, not as he or she wishes it had landed. Swings and clubs, techniques and skills, are changed depending on where the ball is resting. The successful promoter of change understands that you must "do unto others as they want to be done unto". That is, to influence others, you must adapt your approach to fit theirs. You must learn to see the world in their eyes. Knocking on every door with the same opening script creates sore knuckles, not sales. As George Bernard Shaw once said, "It is unwise to do unto others as you would have them do unto you. Their tastes may not be the same."

The person with the most flexibility wins. The Unfair Advantage requires you to put your sail in the other person's wind, to *notice* and to respond with as many different skills as possible.

4. The decision to buy (or trust) is emotional.

The decision to buy is quick and often unrecognized. Frequently, the "buy" decision is not a conscious process. If you think impulse buying is restricted to grocery store checkout counters, you are wrong. Most of your purchase decisions are made on impulse. Your last car or house or even sweater came down to an emotional choice. Even after careful deliberation and analysis prior to any "buy" decision, you still must make a personal decision. And that decision is subjective and emotional and nonconscious. We often refer to it as a "gut" reaction. Only later do we devise a logical rationale to justify our decisions. That rationale can be simple, if we are only justifying to ourselves, or complex if we must justify to someone else. (You should hear me explain to my wife in logical, objective terms why I bought another computer!) We buy in our minds and then we find a logical reason to justify our action.

5. People buy outcomes.

You sell a result—an outcome. People do not buy "oxygen-free copper wire"; they buy better sound for their home theater systems. While the car manufacturers want us to believe that they are making better engineered cars, we still are buying a complex mix of image and transportation. People buy the outcome.

An international consulting firm developed a method for their process of analyzing a business and recommending remedial actions for problems discovered. When they sent a team to sell their program, they began by walking their prospect through each of the many steps of their process. After observing this sales presentation, I realized that no one ever helped the client realize what benefits or outcome they could expect from successfully follow-ing this procedure. Nor did they ever find out what benefits the client might want. They were trying to sell a process, a solution to a non-identified prob-lem. And they were not successful.

Apple Computer launched the Newton with a lot of fanfare and excitement. It was a fascinating piece of design and engineering. The engineers were proud of all the things it did and the state-of-the-art technology it represented. But the customer asked, "What can it do for me?" Unfortunately, the answer was "Not much...but it does it so well."

You cannot sell a method or a process. You cannot sell engineering. You can use all those ideas for helping someone build their justification for making their decision, but method does not sell. People want to know *"What's in it for me?"*

6. There is only one unfair advantage: YOU

There is only one thing that enables you to sell rapport, to adjust to the buying style of the customer, to help the customer develop a rationale after the decision to buy has been made, to help the customer see the benefit to him/her, and ultimately to differentiate you and your idea or service from any other competitor. That one thing is YOU. YOU are the only unfair advantage. People buy you and then they buy your product.

Several years ago I tried to sell The Unfair Advantage workshop to a consulting firm in Chicago. I was told, "We don't sell our services. Our clients buy our services because they recognize our expertise." That consulting practice no longer exists.

Rarely does a buyer differentiate products or services well. The real difference exists in the person doing the selling. You sell yourself first. The buyer buys you first. YOU are the unfair advantage.

BASIC TOOLS OF THE UNFAIR ADVANTAGE

The Unfair Advantage is your ability to make words come alive and have impact, your ability to make people hear and believe. There are two fundamental tools to help you accomplish this.

1. Pace

The best leaders are those who know how to follow. They observe others and take cues from their surroundings to help them lead. They stay in step with those around them and avoid running too far ahead.

The same process holds true for persuasion. First you must learn to follow or *pace* the movements and characteristics of someone before you can introduce change.

The key to rapport is this: *People trust those most like themselves.* The greatest compliment a sales person or consultant can hear is when a customer says "You really speak our language." When you can synchronize yourself with another—or *pace* someone, that person will begin to trust you and assume you see the world as he or she sees it.

Why does perceived similarity lead to trust? It seems to be a simple issue of comfort. People are most comfortable with that which is familiar, whether it be food, music, or human beings. People are most comfortable with others who resemble them. Whether it is skin color, accent, hair length, or voting record, people are more relaxed with those who seem to share a familiar characteristic.

Today, colleges are frustrated by the inability to demonstrate diversity and integration in student bodies. College leaders complain that students still cluster within their racial or ethnic peer groups. Yet no amount of integrated education will ever keep people of similar religions or ethnic backgrounds from grouping together. It is human nature.

Similarly, no amount of education or information will ever keep the single-issue voters of America from supporting single-issue candidates. When there is little else on which to judge, people will accept surface similarities as the basis for trust, even though such a decision will be rationalized and sound more sophisticated when challenged. People will always feel rapport with someone of whom they can say, even on the most superficial of information, "She's one of us."

Pacing is the process of being like another in subtle ways that will not be noticed. If you wear the same clothes as a prospect or try to establish rapport by talking about shared interests, you run the risk of being too obvious. Pacing enables you to accomplish the same results without being obvious or noticed.

Pacing can be accomplished by adjusting your walk or stance to match another, by using similar words or phrases, by adjusting the tone or rate of your speech, and even by subtle posture mirroring. Some of the aspects of a person that can be paced include:

Voice tone and accents
Speech tempo
Figures of speech or phrases

Metaphors
Body posture
Personal values and biases
Interpersonal styles
Individual orientation toward life or time
Linguistic structure

The key to pacing is observing the other person and "becoming" that person at some nonconscious level. Pacing establishes rapport. It is the groundwork for trust and persuasion.

2. Lead

Once you have gained rapport through pacing, you can lead people toward the decision or action you desire.

> *Try this: The next time you are walking with someone, carefully match their pace and rhythm. Maintain this "pacing" for a few minutes. Then gradually increase or decrease the pace. Watch what happens. You will notice that the other person will begin following your lead and unconsciously matching your walk.*

In a similar fashion, you can "move" people with words and mirroring. By pacing and then leading, you can create action and decision.

Leading requires the careful engineering of words to create action. Action words create mental energy. Verbs lead to change. Use them freely. When you can get the mind to think an action, the mental process nearly duplicates the action itself. There is little neurological difference between thinking about running across the street and actually running. This is why the great athletes mentally rehearse their golf swings, high dives, or free throws. If you can use words to get a person to think the action you want them to do, you are on your way to getting what you want. You must lead and not be noticed, however. That is the secret to avoiding resistance. Pace, then lead with your words, and you will have the advantage.

3. Speak the truth

Maintain the integrity of what you are saying. Change the package, not the content, for your audience. The teacher in the movie "The Last Emperor" says it best: "Words are important. If you cannot say what you mean, then you cannot mean what you say, and a gentle man should always mean what he says." Persuasion without integrity cannot be justified. Use your unfair advantage wisely and well.

[1]Paraphrased from Fernando Flores of Action Technologies software firm and author of book on artificial intelligence, Chicago Tribune article by Lamont Wood, November 18, 1990, Understanding Computers and Cognition, Addison-Wesley, 1990,

[2]Johnson, George, In the Palaces of Memory, Alfred A. Knopf, NY, 1991.

[3]We often refer to someone as being "insightful" or having great instincts. In reality, such an individual is probably good at perceiving and knowing how to use filters to increase his/her effectiveness. Such "insight" can be learned.

[4]Reported in Are They Selling Her Lips? by Carol Moog, William Morrow & Co., 1990.

3 The "Engineered Selling Process

> *"Words are, of course, the most powerful drug used by mankind."* —Rudyard Kipling

SELLING IS MORE THAN TELLING

Selling is more than telling, but what exactly is it? What is the process for getting from "meeting-and-greeting" to closing? You have probably seen many of the popular approaches to selling today, from the hard-sell, high-decibel approach used to sell slicer/dicer machines on television to the "consultative selling" or need-based approach encouraged by most business-to-business sales professionals. Most of the better training models emphasize selling to an identified need rather than just telling features and benefits.

But how do you discover the customer's need? Just because *you* think the need exists is not sufficient. The customer must be willing to discuss and carefully look at their needs with you. Unless the customer is willing and ready to interact with you in such an open manner, the consultative selling process cannot occur. Too many contemporary selling models assume the customer or prospect will welcome you and talk freely with you. That assumption is naive.

Before you can identify needs with a customer, you must first create an atmosphere of trust that invites discussion and an exchange of ideas. Such an atmosphere requires a careful balance of rapport building and persuasive leading. Prospects or customers will not simply open themselves to you and share their thoughts and needs, especially in a setting where negotiation and posturing are second nature. A discussion of needs cannot occur until your customer feels comfortable with you and sees you as trustworthy. Before you can discuss benefits or even describe features, before you can identify needs and help solve problems, you must first have a relationship with the prospect. As the relationship is built and reinforced, it is then possible to lead the prospect toward a shared solution and a successful close. *Before you can address needs and act as a consultative seller, you first must sell yourself!*

STEPS IN THE SELLING PROCESS

THE "ENGINEERED" SELLING PROCESS

Get an invitation
Develop the relationship
Exchange information
Maintain relationship
Get a decision

---

1. Get an invitation

Have you ever answered the phone only to hear "*How are you today, sir?*" Instead of inviting conversation, as it supposedly is intended, the result is usually a cool *"Fine"* followed by heightened resistance, because you know what to expect next. You are only waiting for an opening to say *"No thanks, I'm not interested."*

Most people (except telemarketing script writers) immediately recognize the folly of such an approach to selling. Yet the same mistake is made by the eager sales person who starts by asking *"Let me first ask you, how much do you usually spend on photocopy supplies each month?"* or the insurance sales person who greets you with *"You probably think you have enough insurance already, don't you?"* Both of these people, in an attempt to begin a conversation, are actually creating resistance. They are trying to involve the prospect before the prospect is ready.

Typically, you have been given an appointment as the result of contact through mail, telephone, or in person. The successful sales professional needs to understand that an appointment is not an invitation to start a sales pitch. It is merely an invitation to appear.

Even with an appointment, you must get an invitation to sell. That invitation requires a relationship. To get beyond the initial *"Hello"* on the phone or past the handshake in the office, you must begin to establish that relationship. You must quickly develop enough rapport to get "invited" to continue the process of pre-senting yourself and your service or product.

The challenge of getting an invitation is easily seen in retail settings. When the clerk approaches the customer with *"May I help you?"*, he or she is asking for an invitation. Unfortunately, the typical pattern is for the customer to respond, *"No thanks, I'm just looking"*, and the initial opportunity is lost. The successful retail professionals know how to get that invitation by pacing or mirroring the customer, a skill taught later in this book.

In telemarketing, the invitation process is particularly challenging. If you sell over the phone, you usually have less than five seconds to get an invitation to continue. If you are successful, you have earned perhaps as much as 10-15 seconds more before the selling process is threatened. If you try to exceed that time, you will need to seek an additional invitation for more time.

In face-to-face selling, you have a little more time to get the invitation. *But not much!* You must sell yourself within 2-3 minutes or you will not get the invitation to continue. Most sales opportunities fail because the importance of establishing a relationship to earn the "invitation" has been ignored.

2. Develop the relationship

Once you have an invitation to continue, you must develop and strengthen an environment of trust and rapport. The prospect must feel comfortable with you. You can use the skills of The Unfair Advantage to build this relationship quickly and to continue to nurture it. As trust is developed, the prospect will feel comfortable enough to discuss his or her needs.

It is often easier to lose the relationship than to nurture it. If you move too quickly or even too slowly, you can lose the relationship. Resistance is the outcome of this loss. As long as you can keep the relationship alive, you will find little resistance to what you are saying and selling. When you notice resistance, you are being told that the relationship is in jeopardy and it is time to apply some first aid.

3. Exchange information

It is only at this step in the selling process that you can begin "consultative selling." Now, and only now, is the prospect ready to talk about real needs. It is only now that the prospect is ready to listen to the features and benefits you can provide. With rapport established, the exchange of information can be conducted with minimum resistance and a clear commitment to a win/win situation.

This is also when objections occur. Objections are really an opportunity to clarify features and benefits. It is the time to talk about the customer's real needs and concerns. When objections occur in the context of a trusting relationship, they can be handled effectively and efficiently.

NOTE:

The selling process is not a linear process. You do not simply go from step one to step two and onward. It is a constant process of recycling. Frequently, you will discover that the exchange of information, for instance the discussion of price , can create resistance—"Let me think about it." You cannot continue the selling process when you meet such resistance. Instead, you must go BACK to step one and seek an invitation to continue. The selling process requires that you constantly be ready to loop back to the beginning and strengthen the relationship.

---

4. Maintain relationship

In an ideal world, a sale could be achieved immediately following the exchange of information. You have identified needs, you are able to address those needs, and the customer agrees to a deal. Unfortunately, this rarely happens. Instead, issues such as price and delivery dates can lead to tension. When details must be negotiated, the inherent tension can strain a relationship. If the relationship is weakened, comfort levels drop and trust deteriorates. With a drop in trust, people are tempted to hide behind traditional roles of the purchasing agent or savvy buyer. Resistance to a positive solution is intensified.

The way to avoid encouraging such resistance is to remember to work on the relationship before, during, and after the exchange of information. You can build a relationship *while* you are exchanging information. Relationship building and consultative selling are not mutually exclusive activities.

NOTE:

Whenever the relationship is broken, an "invitation" is needed to continue. If, for instance, an objection is not handled well at this stage in the process, it will create resistance. It may then be necessary to go back to the "Invitation" stage to get permission to respond to the objection and continue with the discussion.

---

5. Get a decision (close or get an action toward next step)

The closing step should be the easiest of all. If you have been successful in building rapport and leading the prospect through an effective exchange of ideas, the close will be a logical outcome.

On the other hand, if circumstances prevent closing, then the close becomes another form of maintaining the relationship. You "close" on getting another appointment or another invitation. Or you close on an agreement for action, such as scheduling a time to meet with someone's boss or to present before a committee.

The most important element of the close is to determine *during the selling process* exactly what you want to happen! What decision do you want the prospect or customer to make?

You must have the flexibility to redefine your objective during the selling process.For instance, you may have come in expecting to leave with a contract. However, you then discover that you will be fortunate to leave with a future appointment. Or you may discover that you cannot close on a contract. But you may be able to get an agreement on the specifications of the proposal request, specifications that will favor your product. The top sales professionals are able to redefine the objective quickly. And this skill comes from developing a relationship with the prospect that leads to a good exchange of information.

The selling process is a process of selling yourself. It is also a process of reading your customer and knowing what you can achieve. These are the skills of The Unfair Advantage, and the remainder of this book is dedicated to teaching you how to be successful in the selling process and the process of selling YOU!

4 *Language of the Mind*

"When I use a word," Humpty Dumpty said, in rather a scornful tone, "it means just what I choose it to mean—neither more nor less." "The question is," said Alice, "whether you can make words mean so many different things." "The question is," said Humpty Dumpty, "which is to be master—that's all."—Lewis Carroll, Through the Looking-Glass

Have you ever tried to explain an idea to someone only to realize that you are talking to a brick wall? Then, you hear someone else say nearly the same idea and see an entirely different response? Why did this happen?

Your choice of words can either invite resistance or it can create trust. If you invite resistance, no one will hear your ideas. If you create trust, you gain the confidence of your audience. People will listen to what you say.

Rapport is another word for trust or suspended judgment. You cannot persuade or sell until you are trusted. Before you can create action, the audience must be willing to believe the message. You must be able to create an atmosphere that avoids resistance and distrust. The ability to create rapport by choosing the right words is the most powerful "unfair advantage" in selling and leading.

THE COMMON DENOMINATOR

Sales trainers often tell you to search for what they call the "common denominator" as a way of establishing rapport with a prospect. They suggest you look for an activity or interest that you share with your audience. If you can create an appearance of similarity, the other person is inclined to grant you credibility, at least initially.

The power of the common denominator is one of the foundations of self-help groups such as Alcoholics Anonymous. *"Hello. My name is Fred. I am an alcoholic."* With those words, the speaker is viewed as being "one of us" by the audience. Immediately, trust and believability are granted by the audience to the speaker. People will be inclined to believe the speaker shares their concerns and understands their needs. This is the power of rapport.

In a recent television commercial, a young man and woman are shown on a deck of an outdoor restaurant. The viewer is able to see each of their thoughts. Each is intepreting the scene very differently. Clearly, the two people have little in common. However, the man's discovery of the woman drinking *his* brand of beer leads him to assume immediately that they have much in common.

Although simplistic, the situation modeled in the commercial is nonetheless similar to how you achieve rapport in many situations. People respond to a common denominator, whether it is a drink, the way a person dresses, skin color, or nationality. It is then assumed that values and interests are shared. Trust is initially granted.

FAILURE OF THE COMMON DENOMINATOR APPROACH

However, the search for the common denominator as a way to establish rapport is usually ineffective with most sales professionals. The reason for its failure is simple: IT IS TOO OBVIOUS. When a sales person enters your office, notices a picture of a fishing expedition on your shelf and begins to talk about how she loves to fish, you immediately become suspicious of her sincerity. You smell manipulation and you become increasingly resistant and doubtful. Instead of building rapport, this approach actually increases resistance.

What is needed is a way of creating the sensation of similiarity, the common denominator, the *Hello, My name is Fred*, without being so obvious. This can be done by mirroring the "Language of the Mind." Your choice of words can determine if someone feels comfortable with you or feels uneasy in your presence.

THE LANGUAGE OF THE MIND

The words you use to speak or write and even the thoughts you use to talk to yourself are not randomly chosen. There is a reason why you choose one word over another, although in most cases the reason is a nonconscious one.

Similarly, you like to hear familiar words and phrases. You are more responsive and receptive when you are hearing or reading words that are part of your normal life. When someone speaks your language, you are more likely to respond. Have you ever noticed how easy it is to hear someone speaking your native tongue when you are in a foreign country, even when you are in a crowd of people?

When your words are different from those of your audience, people react. Sometimes they see the obvious and resent your ignorance, such as when you speak English and they speak French. A comment often heard in Europe is, *"That crazy American. He's been in the country five years and the only word in our language he can speak is 'OK'."*

Other times, your words may simply be unfamiliar, like an engineer trying to talk to watercolor artists. Something about your words fails to create a sense of comfort for them, and this discomfort is extended to include their feelings about you.

Yet, few of us consciously and purposefully notice the language differences around us every day. Notice the tension created in the following conversation:

> Jane: *"If you look over that copy again, you will see clearly that I have focused on all the things that needed to be highlighted. I hope you can see what a great picture it presents of the situation."*
>
> John: *"It has impact alright, but I just get the feeling that something is out of place. It doesn't hit me right.*
>
> Jane: *"Maybe you just aren't viewing it in the right light. Try to look at it from a different perspective, from what the buyer will be looking for. Can't you just see the potential?"*

This is an exchange of sincere comments that inadvertently creates tension. Jane and John are not speaking the same language. Each is probably concentrating on the message and ignoring how it is said. By ignoring language, they are creating tension, and tension is getting in the way of the message being heard. The words, not the message, are creating what is sometimes labeled as "resistance" or "defensiveness."

All people have a preference in their choice of words and verbal style. When they receive a message that reflects or mirrors their language preference, they feel more comfortable and more willing to accept both the message and the sender.

Your choice of words, especially verbs and predicates, is the direct result of the sensory pathway that is the strongest

33

and most developed for you. These are the words you absorb most quickly when you read or hear them, and they are the words that come to you most easily when you want to express an idea, especially when you are in a hurry and do not want to think about how you are saying what you are saying. This preferred set of words forms a vocabulary or language that is labeled in NLP as a "lead" system or preferred language. It is the language in which you prefer to think as well as speak. It is your preferred language of the mind!

Everyone has a preferred language. Your lead system is the language YOU prefer. It is the one that sounds best to you in an ad or seems most effective in a letter. However, just because it is your preferred language does not mean it is better than any other set of words. It just happens to fit YOU.

EXERCISE

Language Preference

Consider the following descriptions of a house. Pretend for a moment that you are in the market to buy a house. Which of these houses interests you most?

House 1 is picturesque in its discriminating splendor. As you look around the outside of the house, you will see that care has been taken to ensure year-round color, with trees, ground-cover, and bushes that will always add brilliant hues and contrast wherever you look, whatever the season may be. It has a bright sunny layout. You will recognize this as a home with a welcome glow all about.

House 2 beckons you in a subtle and quiet way. Yet is seems to make a statement about comfortable and gracious living. It is in a quiet area away from the noise of the city. But soon you will find yourself talking about this house in a special way. Its interior has been hailed as unique. You can quickly tell it has been well maintained like a fine-tuned engine, and the grounds and added specials speak for themselves. It has the features that most people ask for in this type of house and we are told that few can match this builder for a quality reputation.

House 3 is well constructed by a firm with a solid reputation. Its warmth is conveyed through the many unique touches added to it by sensitive previous owners. It has room to move yet you feel

35

immediately restful within its well-designed living space. It has a garden area to let you get your hands dirty, yet space enough for just walking around and enjoying the sense of country living. It is well-built, and the construction can easily withstand nature's onslaughts from high winds to freezing temperatures without having an impact on your comfort inside. This is a house that will grow on you quickly, and you will soon feel as if it fits like a warm and comfortable glove.

After reading the three house descriptions, which interested you more? Did you have a clear favorite? Did you also notice that at least one house actually held so little interest for you that you probably skipped words and hurried to the next paragraph?

If all words were equally persuasive, you would not have noticed any difference in your reaction to the three descriptions. But that is not what happened, is it? You probably preferred one over the others. Or at least, you found one description completely lacking in qualities that interested you.

Yet the above paragraphs were descriptions of the same house. Only the words were different!

What you may find surprising is to learn that your choice of the most interesting or effective description of the house is not the same as everyone else's! For instance, in The Unfair Advantage workshop, I have asked over 700 CEOs of small to medium-sized companies throughout the United States to indicate their preferred house description. The number voting for House #1, #2, or #3 is about even. No one description is best, yet nearly every one of the 700 executives had a preference.

So why did you choose one description as being more interesting? One description "spoke" to you more clearly than another. It may have helped you visualize the house or it made you feel more comfortable. Whatever your subjective experience, one set of words had a better impact on you than the other two. Those words matched you.

Listening or hearing or even reading is a selective process. Not everyone hears or sees the same things. Several people can witness a crime and not agree on what they saw. A jury can hear the evidence and not agree on the conclusion. You will see something useful in this chapter that will be different from what another reader will pick up.

The influence of language preference is profound. Not only do words influence your trust level with someone, they also influence what messages get through your nonconscious filter. Word choices help determine what you read, hear, or remember. One key to selling is to use the "best" words for your audience.

THE "BEST" WORDS TO USE

Because people prefer their own language, they often judge a different language as inferior. Have you ever tried to write a news release or a memo with a committee? Why is it often so difficult to write ad copy that the client and the creative staff can agree on?

Suppose you are trying to write a tag line for an advertisement for a long-distance phone service. Which are the BEST words to use?

> *"PhoneCo lets you keep in* touch *with those* you love *and* miss. *"*
>
> *"PhoneCo...you will immediately* see *the difference from your first call."*
>
> *"PhoneCo...so* clear *it's as if you were* whispering *in their* ear. *"*

The answer? There are no BEST words for everyone.

"Best" depends on your audience. What works for one person may not work for another. The only way to answer *"Which is best?"* is to respond *"For whom?"*

People respond to words that fit them. If the words are the right ones for them, people will hear the message. The right words will jump out from a page of print. But the "best" words for you are only "best" for YOU. They may not be "best" for someone else. (For a hint at your preferred language, see the LPI test in the Addendum.)

LANGUAGE PREFERENCE CODES (VAK)

Language "preference" is revealed by the action words (verbs and predicates) you tend to choose at any given time. Those words reveal the way you are processing information (thinking) at the moment.

> *"I see what is going on here."*
> *"I hear the problem and would like to say something about it."*
> *"I get a feeling that something is happening here."*
> *"There is a strange smell to this situation."*
> *"That proposal leaves a funny taste in my mouth."*

Reflecting the primary five senses, a language can be labeled according to the sensory path that has the dominant role in a person's choice of words:

Visual (*"I see your point"*)
Auditory (*"I hear you"*)
Kinesthetic (*"I don't have a good feel for that yet"*)
Olfactory (*"Something smells here"*)
Gustatory (*"Oh, that is sweet"*)

In Western cultures, however, there are few words to express ideas in the Olfactory and Gustatory language. Therefore, the majority of sensory-based words used by Western speakers and writers can be labeled *V (visual), A (auditory),* or *K (kinesthetic, feel/touch).*

A Visual person is someone who tends to prefer to use the eyes for perceiving as well as for remembering and thinking. An Auditory person tends to use listening, hearing, and speaking as preferred ways of noticing and learning. The Kinesthetic person is apt to rely on what he or she may call intuition as well as the sense of touch to relate to the world.

When people are asked to justify their choice of the "best" house description in the exercise above, their choice of words typically match the language of the paragraph.

> *"I liked paragraph one the best. I could <u>see</u> myself in that house, and it made me think of the way my house <u>looks</u> to me. (V)"*
>
> *"Paragraph two is the one I prefer. It <u>sounds</u> like the way I <u>talk</u> about a house I like. (A)"*
>
> *"I <u>feel</u> better about paragraph three. It seems to <u>fit</u> my style better. (K)"*

There is also a Digital or Conceptual language. Digital is actually a non-sensory language, that is, unrelated to any sensory activity. Digital words are unrelated to the speaker's/writer's sensory system and also fail to stimulate sensory activity in the audience. They simply fill space.

The Digital language is used when the speaker is not interacting and only wants to be telling. Too often, it is a vocabulary for people who are more concerned with sounding good than with saying something meaningful. They are the favorite words of politicians, lawyers, and consultants who are trying to impress:

"Pursuant to your inquiry, the parties involved are reviewing their options and considering appropriate responses."

"A downsizing is indicated, judging from the under-utilized resources and the lack of empowerment within the human resources network."

"While an affirmative vote might be indicated, the needs of the constituents preclude such a decision until more consideration is given to the multitude of issues involved."

People speak in Digital words when they rely on jargon or "sound bites" to express themselves with prepared answers or memorized slogans. Digital phrases often lose any real meaning and become substitutes for more in-depth analysis. Digital words, especially technical jargon, can sometimes help you gain credibility with others in your profession, but they *never* help you persuade or develop trust.

Many business people as well as lawyers and consultants act as if Digital words sound more "business-like." This is only true if "business-like" means boring and lacking in impact. In short, Digital words often impress the speaker more than they persuade the listener. Small wonder people fall asleep during speeches when someone is trying to sound "business-like".

Most people use all three languages in expressing themselves. Under pressure, however, one sensory language is usually preferred over the other two, and if the stress is particularly high, they may choose the one language to exclusion of the other two. (For instance, you may know a Visual person who, under stress, finds it impossible to listen to suggestions or comments from others, because he/she "sees" clearly what needs to be done to solve the crisis.)

During non-stress times, your language preference may be less obvious. Most people are comfortable with a mix of languages and will move from one sensory-based set of words to another with ease. Depending on the topic, your preference may change from visual to auditory, for instance. You may be visual when you write but kinesthetic when you talk. You may be kinesthetic when you talk about buying a car and visual when you choose clothes. All people have a lead system, however, and it is important for you to recognize that your preferred language may not be the same as the person next to you.

IDENTIFYING LANGUAGE PREFERENCES

When Bill Clinton says, "I feel your pain," he reveals his preference for the Kinesthetic language. On the other hand, George H.W. Bush ("Thousand points of light") was often ridiculed for his verbal style. A Visual, he would often visualize his idea and say only parts of what he was thinking, because the concept always seemed clear and fully formed to him. Without verbalizing the context which was in his head, the listener was left with a shorthand version that often lacked clarity. Richard Nixon, an Auditory, whose downfall was ironically hastened by audio tapes, was famous for his *Let me say this about that…*

Sometimes, you can identify a person's language preference by watching carefully what interests them. A Kinesthetic will play with a brochure or sample of your product, even when your discussion has moved on to something else. A Visual may stare at a piece of paper without really seeming to focus. An Auditory may read the headings and the summary but will expect you to fill in the blanks with discussion. Careful observation can sometimes give you a clue to a person's preferred language.

41

> *A vegetable wholesaler once told me he could label his buyers according to their Visual, Auditory, or Kinesthetic preferences. He said the Visual buyers would look at a lot of peas, for example, and never touch them. They would stare, look at color and texture, and make a decision. The Auditory buyers would put a sample in their mouth and listen to the crunch as they bit down. The Kinesthetics would take a sample, roll it around in their fingers, and maybe even smash it between their fingers. All of this behavior would take place before the decision to buy would be made.*

It is often impossible to judge a person's language preference from their writing. Unless they write exactly as they speak, assumptions about preference can be risky. People often write as they have been taught to write, rather than write as they think. They want to sound "business-like." This is the source of most Digital words. Unless you know someone writes exactly as he/she talks, it is not usually helpful to try to plan your selling approach based on written documents.

> *A CEO of a small manufacturing business told me he had hired a speech-writer to help him with his heavy writing load. However, he had begun to notice that she extensively re-wrote everything he gave her. At first, he feared he was losing his verbal skills. Eventually he discovered he wrote with a heavy preference for Visual words. She was rewriting everything to reflect her strong Auditory preference!*

Advertising and marketing efforts are intended to persuade you to buy. Yet, expensive campaigns are frequently launched without considering language preferences as one way to increase the appeal to the customer. They most likely reveal the preference of the creative person behind the scenes. Can you label the language preference in the following examples?

"A little voice tells you to buy NHT"
"I can see you in an Eagle Talon"
"You can hear a pin drop."
"Reach out and touch someone."
"Must see TV. NBC."
"Big Mac attack"
"Mazda-it just feels right."
"When you care enough to send the very best."

You can sometimes identify language preference even when your audience is not talking. You can identify language preference if you notice when someone seems to perk up, to pay closer attention to one language over another. A good observer can notice which language prompts the most active response. When this is observed, your language can be adjusted to fit the listener.

A public relations firm in Chicago often makes formal proposals to committees. After an Unfair Advantage workshop, the team leader described a recent presentation:

"We began our presentation, but the buyer refused to look at any of us. She was trying to intimidate us and was doing a good job at it. However, I noticed that whenever one of our team spoke for a few seconds using Visual words, the buyer would look up briefly. So, when I stood to do my part of the presentation, I spoke almost entirely in Visual words. I was able to establish eye contact with her and she began to warm to our ideas and ask

43

questions. It was the first time we had achieved any dialogue at all with her. We also got her approval for the campaign."

Once you learn to notice language preferences, you are ready to *pace* or match that language. The next chapter will give you more ideas for language pacing.

5 *Language Pacing*

"Words—so innocent and powerless as they are, as standing in a dictionary, how potent they become in the hands of one who knows how to combine them." —Nathaniel Hawthorne

LANGUAGE MIRRORING OR PACING

One of the nicest thing clients or customers can say to you is *"You really speak our language."* It means they believe you understand them and you seem to have insight into their needs. It means they trust you!

To get that trust, you must know how to listen. But simply saying *"Listen better"* does not really help, does it? All you have to do is remember your school years to see that being told *"Be a better listener"* is not particularly useful advice. If you want to have an unfair advantage, you need to know what to listen for and what to do with that information. This skill is called language pacing or language mirroring. (Both terms are used interchangeably in NLP.)

You gain the advantage when you gain trust. And trust can be achieved quickly by listening and choosing your words carefully. You want to actually *speak* the other person's lan-

guage by choosing words that match your audience's preference for Visual, Auditory, or Kinesthetic words. When you
can adjust your words to match the preference of your listener,
you create rapport and gain their trust unconsciously.

When you ignore language preferences, you invite tension.
Imagine someone trying to sell this house:

> *Realtor: "I **saw** a great house for you yesterday
> in the Bellwood area. It is a gorgeous development."*
> (Visual language preference)
> *Buyer: "I don't know. I think I may have **heard**
> some things about Bellwood. What do you say we
> **talk** about some other options first?"* (Auditory
> language preference)
> *Realtor: "Oh, but this place **looks** like just the
> house. It is beautiful. How can you not want to
> **see** it?"* (Visual language preference)

Can you hear the conflict in this exchange? Instead of responding to the customer and moving toward a sale, the realtor
has introduced a barrier to the selling situation by failing to
see the buyer's preferred Auditory language.

Consider how much more effective she would have been if
the following had been the interaction:

> *Realtor: "I **saw** a great house for you yesterday
> in the Bellwood area. It is a gorgeous development."*
> (Visual)
> *Buyer: "I don't know. I think I may have **heard**
> some things about Bellwood. What do you say we
> **talk** about some other options first?"* (Auditory)
> *Realtor: "Let's **talk** about what you've heard,*

*because it **sounds** as if you may have been misinformed. I can **call** some people who live there and you can **discuss** it with them. If you then **tell** me your concerns are gone, I want you to **listen** to more about the place I mentioned. Otherwise, I'll **change my tune** and we'll **talk** about some other options.* " (Auditory)

In the second example, the realtor recognized the Auditory language preference of the buyer. She adjusted her words to match the buyer's preferred language.

This adjustment is the skill of language pacing. You are choosing words that match the other person's language preference. By mirroring the buyer's preferred language, an unconscious process occurs that makes the buyer more comfortable with the realtor. Trust is enhanced when the realtor speaks the buyer's language.

When the words someone uses do not fit the words you prefer to hear or read, you unconsciously resist, regardless of the content.

I recently read a brochure that was filled with phrases like "rewarding relationship", "solid support", "superior service", *and* "competitive capabilities combining strength..." *It also made frequent reference to the company's* "continuing dialogue", "the voices of the forgotten", *and their determination to* "talk bottom line" *and* "talk straight". There was little question that the copy was prepared by an Auditory. What do you think a Kinesthetic did with that brochure? Read it (V)? Hear its message (A)? Throw it out (K)? Who was intended audience?

Similarly, people notice and remember the words that fit them. The phrase *"We will go to any length to serve you"* may be virtually ignored by the same person who will respond positively to *"We look for new ways to serve you."* While the message is the same, it will be missed if the wrong words are used. A person who prefers using Visual words will be more comfortable listening to Visual words and may not notice a Kinesthetic message. People respond more quickly and sometimes unconsciously to their preferred language while often ignoring and even resisting words that do not fit with their preference.

> *Ralph, the CEO of a small manufacturing firm and Larry, the CFO, were constantly at odds. They both attended a management meeting one morning. Larry brought stacks of printouts and graphs. After pouring over the data, the meeting was adjourned. Two hours later, there was a loud commotion in the hall. Ralph was yelling, "Why didn't you tell me there was a problem like this?"*
>
> *Larry responded, "I did. I showed you three different analyses and several graphs that all displayed this problem. It was easy to see the problem right there in front of your face!"*
>
> *"You and your computer printouts!" said Ralph, "If we had a problem, why didn't you tell me? That's your job, you know, to make sure I hear about developing problems."*

Can you identify the language preferences? How could this whole misunderstanding have been avoided?

Everyone has a preferred way of speaking, hearing, and seeing an idea. This is true if the person is reading the language or hearing it. People prefer to read and hear the language that fits their own personal preference. For that person, the "best" wording at any given time may be different from your own preferred way of speaking or writing.

The key to language pacing is to *hear* the cues and to *translate* your message into the other person's preferred language. On the following pages, you will find examples of words and phrases that represent Visual, Auditory, and Kinesthetic languages.

VISUAL LANGUAGE Examples

aim	foggy	look	show
appear	gaze	luster	sight
behold	glance at	murky	sparkle
blind	glare	observe	stain
blush	gleam	oversight	stare
bright	glimpse	panorama	study
brilliant	glisten	pattern	sunny
cloudy	glow	picture	view
dark	hazy	portray	viewpoint
dim	illuminate	pretty	visible
draw	image	reveal	vision
dull	light	scan	vista
faded	likeness	see	watch

VISUAL Phrases

Look at this

Visualize the idea

See it

Picture this scenario

Focus on this

What is the perspective

Let's scan this

Watch this

Observe that

Paint a picture

Show me

Picture the following

Gaze at that

Preview the outline

Draw conclusions

Map out the plan

The picture is cloudy

A strategic vision

Dark side

Glowing review

Shed light on the issue

Obscure the view

Colorful presentation

Brighter prospect

Light at the end of the tunnel

Don't tell me...write it

Look into it

AUDITORY LANGUAGE Examples

articulate	declare	mutter	sing
aloud	describe	narrate	sound
amplify	discuss	noise	sounds like
announce	dissonance	noisy	speak
argue	eavesdrop	order	speech
babble	express	praise	squawk
blaring	groan	purr	talk
boom	grumble	quiet	tell
call	harmony	remark	thunderous
chat	hear	resound	told
chatter	hiss	ring	tone
chime	lecture	say	tune
clatter	lend an ear	scream	utter
comment	listen	shout	verbalize
conversation	loud	shriek	vocalize
converse	mention	shrill	voice
cry out	moan	silence	

AUDITORY Phrases

Sounds good	We are in harmony
I hear you	It rings true
Let's talk about it	Sing their praises
Tell about that	They are tuning out
Call me	Echo their sentiments
Let me tell you	Scream to be heard
Lend an ear	Amplify that point
It's a whisper	It purred like a kitten
Loud and clear	The silent treatment
Don't give me static	Chime in
I'm in tune with that	Debate the issue
Tone of conversation	Don't grumble
Voice your opinion	Argue the point
Ask them	

KINESTHETIC LANGUAGE Examples

absorb	fear	push	support
attach	feel	ragged	tackle
attack	firm	reach	take
backing	flat	relaxed	tender
balance	flush	resist	tension
bend	fumble	rough	throw
catch	grab	rugged	tickle
cold	grasp	seize	tight
compress	hard	sense	touch
concrete	hot	shake up	tremble
connect	hurt	shocking	twist
cool	itch	shuffle	unbalance
cram	link	solid	uncomfortable
cut	massage	stable	unite
cutting	merge	steady	weigh
exhale	nervous	stiff	worry
extend	point	stir	
fall	pressure	stretch	
fasten	probe	sturdy	

KINESTHETIC Phrases

Get a feel for	Make it tangible
Too hot to handle	What is the impact
Kick it upstairs	Tickle it out
Ill-at-ease	Manipulate the data
It scares me	A solid base
Point it out	Tough to deal with
Stir it up	Merge our ideas
Toss this around	Make a connection
I'm not comfortable	Stop talking...do it
It worries me	Back up your claim
A concrete idea	Cut through
Go for it	Open up
It irritates me	Push through

DIGITAL LANGUAGE Examples

accommodate –	engage	inquiry	regard
analyze —	engross	judge	remember
believe	estimate	know	respond
benefit	establish	learn	results
capability	evaluate	materialize	service
change	experience	motivate	think
circumstances	facilitate	need	understand
comprehend	fascinate	negotiate	utilize
conjecture	guess	ponder	want
consider –	hypothesize	pretend	wonder
contemplate	ideas	process	
convey	identify	professional	(plus: most
credibility	imagine	produce	words with
decide	intellectual-	qualify	3 syllables or
deem	ize	quality	more!!!)
deliberate	interest	recognize	

DIGITAL Phrases

In regard to your concern...

We are considering the
following possibilities...

An interesting dilemma

A viable solution

As we analyze the potentiality...

Consider the options

Value quality

Promote a philosophy

The functionality

Think about it

53

> **NOTE:**
>
> It is a good idea to code routinely all phone inquiries: V..A..K..(Visual, Auditory, Kinesthetic). In this way, if you need to persuade or sell, you then will know how to get rapport and create an atmosphere that invites more information from the caller. This coding process is not as hard as it may sound. The mind works much faster than a person can talk, and with practice, you can easily code a conversation and not miss the flow of the discussion. (See coding exercise on Page 68.)

PACING VISUALS

People who prefer the Visual Language use words such as *see, look,* or *picture.* Look at the list on Page 50 for examples of Visual Language words that can be cues to the person's language preference. Phrases also can be cues. Phrases such as *"illustrate a point"* or *"brighter prospect"* are Visual phrases.

To pace someone's words or phrases, simply use the same language preference. When someone says, *"Let's take a closer look at that issue",* you want to respond with a Visual phrase, such as *"I think I can show you..."* Or *"Maybe this will throw some light on it..."*

> *One day, I was called by a prospect I had pursued for a long time. After a few pleasantries, he began, "How do you see your training program?"*

The use of "see," a visual language cue, was consistent with his opening remarks and helped me decide his predominant language was Visual.

Unfortunately, my preferred language for describing my workshop was not Visual. As a result, I found myself limited to using phrases such as "It looks like...", "You'll see...", and "Try to picture..."

Even though I was struggling, since I was using his preferred language, he did not notice my repetition or limited vocabulary. In fact, he was very comfortable with my choice of words. After all, they were his choice!

But the results were clear. First, the prospect did most of the talking. He became extremely enthusiastic about what he was hearing (or should I say seeing in his mind?) and he kept expanding the possibilities bigger and bigger. To keep him talking and to keep him selling himself, I occasionally said, "See what you think of this...," "It looks like...", or "Picture this.." Within a short time, he saw how well the program matched his mental image of what he wanted.

Another sign that a person has a Visual preference is to notice how easily the person gets distracted by things about the room. If you notice your prospect or customer tends to follow your hands when you gesture, this may be a clue that the person has a Visual preference.

Visuals have a tendency to be poor listeners. The Visual will begin to visualize a concept and drift away from you. When this occurs, the Visual may be left with an image of your idea that does not match yours. It is necessary to retrace steps and frequently check for consistency with Visuals.

Still another clue that a person is a Visual is the occasional choppy or incomplete phrases you may hear. Visuals tend to get ideas as complete images. Consequently, when trying to express the idea, they may leave out words and part of the image in their head. George Bush Sr. was frequently the brunt of jokes by cartoonists for his strange comments. Yet, it is certain President Bush had a complete image of his idea in his head. He simply failed to verbalize the whole picture to his audience, unaware that others could not *see* what he was thinking. This is a frequent problem for Visuals.

NOTE:

When trying to sell or counsel to a Visual, it is important, of course, to match his/her language. Use Visual words. It also helps to use lists, graphs, or pictures to make your point. Help the person SEE the possibilities and the outcomes. (Self-affirmations do not work well with Visuals. Surprised?)

56

EXERCISE

Visual Pacing

Write or say the following ideas using Visual Language:

1. It's a good idea, but it needs some changing.

2. Do you get my point?

3. We have a great product that will help your productivity.

Sample responses:

1. It's a good idea, but it needs some changing.
     V: *I like the way this looks, but we could probably polish it up a bit more.*

2. Do you get my point?
     V: *Can you see what I am saying?*

3. We have a great product that will help your productivity.
     V: *What I am going to show you will get you closer to that vision you have for your people.*

57

PACING AUDITORIES

People who prefer the Auditory language use words such as *hear* or *sounds like*. Look at the list on Page 51 for examples of Auditory Language examples that can be cues to the person's language preference. Word phrases can also be cues. Phrases such as *"Sounds good to me"* or *"That rings true"* are Auditory phrases.

People who prefer the Auditory language often enjoy the sound of their own voice. They can be good listeners, but they may have a tendency to talk too much.

Auditories can sometimes be noticed by their frequent use of alliterations, rhythmic phrases or rhymes. *"We found friendship and fellowship in the freedom we shared"* is likely something said by an Auditory.

Auditories can motivate themselves with self-affirmations. Many self-motivation books are aimed at Auditories, especially those packaged as audio tapes. "Positive Mental Attitude", "The Power of Positive Thinking", and the <u>Inner Game of</u>...series are all examples of approaches to "self-talk" that are very useful for Auditories.

Similarly, if you want to sell Auditories, you need to talk to them. Give them explanations and opportunities for dialogue. They are not apt to read the manual or study your written materials, unless you can link that material to something you said in your discussions with them. They often are influenced, too, by quotes or advice from others whom they respect.

NOTE:

When selling an Auditory, tell them what others have said about your service or product. When possible, provide them with an audio tape that tells your story. Vocal pacing of tone and other vocal characteristics can be especially effective with Auditories. And use the phone frequently and effectively to stay in touch, or more accurately, in "voice."

EXERCISE

Auditory Pacing

Write or say the following ideas using Auditory Language:

1. It's a good idea, but it needs some changing.

2. Do you get my point?

3. We have a great product that will help your productivity.

Sample responses:

1. It's a good idea, but it needs some changing.
   A: I like the sound of it, but we need to talk it over a bit more.

2. Do you get my point?
   A: Do you hear what I am saying?

3. We have a great product that will help your productivity.
   A: People tell us we help create a productive environment that gets everyone singing from the same page. Sound like something worth talking about?

60

PACING KINESTHETICS

People who prefer the Kinesthetic language use words such as *push, grab, kick,* and *stretch.* Look at the list on Page 52 for examples of Kinesthetic Language that can be cues to the person's preference. Phrases can also be cues. Phrases such as *"Let's get the ball rolling"* or *"That feels right"* are Kinesthetic phrases.

>   *A friend of mine received a direct mail piece from a marketing group. The package included a miniature bicycle-built-for-two. This group was very proud of how it helped people "get in touch" with their message, they said. The bike had a sign that read: "We work in tandem with our clients." The letter consisted of strong phrases such as "..working in partnership", "...message to be delivered and absorbed by clients...", "...creative and dramatic...", and "...designed and executed."*

>   *Unfortunately, my friend is Visual. He took the lovely bicycle and put it on his shelf of knick-knacks in front of his desk. In less than a few weeks, he had completely forgotten the source of the bike or the message that was sent with it.*

>   *Shortly after receiving the bike, he also received a promotion piece from a different company. This package consisted of an inexpensive slide viewer with a slide of some marketing executives receiving an award. The letter said they would like to see if they could meet with and show some of their work to him. THEY received an appointment within a few days! Coincidence? Or an example of the power of language matching?!*

Kinesthetics are feeling-oriented. Bill Clinton's "*I can feel your pain*" and the ease with which tears would well up in his eyes in public are examples of typical kinesthetic behavior.

Kinesthetics also need to feel a situation before they can understand it fully. Consequently, they may ask what appears to be the same question over and over until they can generate an internal reaction or connection to what is being said. They are also quick to perceive tension around them.

Kinesthetics tend to have a short attention span. They often become acutely aware of a need to move or stand up after sitting in a meeting for too long. The advice to speakers to never speak longer than 45 minutes without a break was probably developed as a reaction to Kinesthetics. (I have recently developed an online series of lessons, The Ten-Minute Advantage, because Kinesthetics do not seem to want to spend longer than that with an online lesson.)

Kinesthetics often like to touch. They are inclined to be more physical and more intrusive of "space" than others. Kinesthetics must guard against this natural tendency, however, in this day of political correctness and sensitivity to anything that could be construed to be inappropriate.

When negotiating with Kinesthetics, they may tend to *feel* a deal is done before the details are well developed. Visuals and Auditories are sometimes frustrated by the lack of details in such situations. They want to see or hear the specifics. The Kinesthetics often let others handle such details.

NOTE:

When selling to Kinesthetics, try to give them something to touch or manipulate. Try to meet them face-to-face; otherwise, you may not be able to tell when they have drifted off into their own thoughts and feelings. Keep active with Kinesthetics by physically marking on brochures or business cards, moving material around, etc.

EXERCISE

Kinesthetic Pacing

Write or say the following ideas using Kinesthetic Language:

1. It's a good idea, but it needs some changing.

2. Do you get my point?

3. We have a great product that will help your productivity.

Sample responses:

1. It's a good idea, but it needs some changing.
   A: It feels OK, but let's iron out a few wrinkles.

2. Do you get what I'm trying to tell you?
   A: Are you catching this? Do you feel my concern about this issue?

3. We have a great product that will help your productivity.
   A: Our product will boost your productivity and raise the bar for what you think people can do! It will knock you over.

DIGITAL PACING

It may seem unusual to think about pacing Digital language. It has already been said that Digital words do not create rapport and are not connected to the thinking process. However, in some businesses, people *expect* you to sound Digital, and if you avoid it, your credibility will be questioned.

> **NOTE:**
>
> Digital pacing does NOT lead to action nor does it create initial rapport. It should not be used to start the rapport building in the Selling Process. However, once initial trust has been established, Digital pacing can help the customer *rationalize* why he or she is feeling comfortable with you. The decision to buy is non-conscious, but the subsequent rationalization can benefit from your pacing jargon or buzz-words that are likely to be Digital. Use such pacing with caution, however, because Digital pacing CANNOT SUSTAIN rapport. It will get stuffy, and you will lose your rapport.
>
> For best results, use the following pattern:
> 1. Pace V, A, or K for rapport
> 2. Insert Digital for credibility
> 3. Return to VAK pacing to recover rapport

For instance, engineers must use the jargon of their business with other engineering-oriented customers. Manufacturing people expect to hear you talk about JIT, ISO9001, or other similar familiar words. If a computer salesperson does not work "RAM" or USB into a conversation, someone may suspect he/she does not understand the product.

Choose your words to match the language preference of the person you are trying to influence. Your words can be a powerful tool for building trust. People will talk more freely with less personal filtering of your ideas. They will also be more inclined to follow your lead.

> *A department manager was advertising for a supervisor. She had received nearly 120 resumes. Preferring an Auditory language, she was having difficulty motivating herself to study the resumes. An internal candidate understood the problem. She called the manager and <u>read</u> her resume over the phone, adding that she would send the paper for follow-up discussion. She got the job!*

When you are not getting the reaction you want, you know it is time to change your language. For instance, in a meeting, which phrases do you use?

> *Does anyone see a problem here?*
> *Is there something we need to talk more about?*
> *How do you feel about this proposal?*

If you notice you are not getting the response you would like, try changing your words. Instead of *"Does anyone see a problem here?"*, change your words to *"Have you heard anything that may cause a problem?"* or *"Anything here make you uncomfortable?"*. Notice that the first question was Visual and was changed to Auditory and then to Kinesthetic. You can safely use all three phrases without risk of your audience noticing the redundancy. People tend to notice only those words which fit their language preference.

Language pacing is the ability to put your ideas into someone else's words. People hear and respond fastest to their preferred language. They also offer less resistance when an idea is expressed in their language. If you want people to hear what you have to say, your words must speak to THEM as if you were talking only to them. When someone looks at what you write, you want to know that those words will be seen and will get through the rest of the fog that competes for attention. You must know how to make words work for you. The person with the most flexibility wins.

> **NOTE:**
>
> **When you are using a language that is not your preference, you will not be smooth or elegant. In fact, you will probably be clumsy and somewhat tongue-tied. It does not matter. When you are pacing another person, that person will feel comfortable with you and your words. Your own discomfort makes no difference. You can be effective without being very good at this skill! Practice will make you smoother. But pacing works without your having to have a rich vocabulary in the other person's language. Simplicity will still get results.**

67

EXERCISE

Language Preference Identification

Identify the language of the following phrases--Are they visual (V), auditory (A), kinesthetic (K), or digital (D)?

1. This issue is too hot to handle.   —

2. I look forward to our meeting.   —

3. Much has been said about our service.   —

4. Listen carefully to what we are showing you.   —

5. How can we clear this matter up?   —

6. I understand.   —

7. If you can tell yourself that what you have seen makes sense, then we have been successful.   —

8. If you can see how this can work for you, speak up now.   —

9. When you care enough to send the very best.   —

(Answers on next page)

Language Preference Identification Exercise:
Sample Answers

Identify the language of the following phrases--Are they visual (V), auditory (A), kinesthetic (K), or digital (D)?

1. This issue is too hot to handle. <u>K</u>

2. I look forward to our meeting. <u>V</u>

3. Much has been said about our service. <u>A</u>

4. Listen carefully to what we are showing you. <u>A, (V or K*)</u>

5. How can we clear this matter up? <u>K*or A or V</u>

6. I understand. <u>D</u>

7. If you can tell yourself that what you have seen makes sense, then we have been successful. <u>A, V, K</u>

8. If you can see how this can work for you, speak up now. <u>V, K, A</u>

9. When you care enough to send the very best. <u>K</u>

*Some words are vague and can be coded several ways, depending on YOUR bias. Try to avoid such words when you are trying to have the maximum influence on your audience.

EXERCISE

Language Flexibility

Answer the following question:

Why should I buy your product/service/idea?

Limit your vocabulary to the language indicated. In other words, your first response will be to a Visual person.

VISUAL:

AUDITORY:

KINESTHETIC:

(Examples on next page.)

Language Flexibility Exercise:
Sample Answers

"Why should I buy your product/service/idea?

Visual: *You only need to take a close **look** at this widget. Notice how **shiny** the finish is. You will **see** we give the same attention to the machining inside. Let me **show** you...*

Auditory: *I can **tell** you my reasons. But maybe you would rather **hear** what other people **say** about us. It does not take long to discover that these endorsements **ring** true...*

Kinesthetic: *Deciding to **buy** is a **gut feeling** sometimes--a matter of **trust**. But I want to **give** you more than just a feeling to help you **want** our widgets...*

71

6 Addressing a VAK-Mixed Audience

"For those who yearn to be free...America is not just a word, it is hope, a torch shedding light to all the hopeless of the world."
—Ronald Reagan, Quoted in Richard Perloff's The Dynamics of Persuasion, p. 176.

INTRODUCTION

Addressing an unknown audience is a unique challenge. You cannot guess their language preference. I have a form letter on my desk that begins, "Dear reader, I have a montage picture of you in my mind's eye. I **see** you running an independent business...(Or) maybe your business is so far just a **gleam in your eye**." (Emphasis is mine.)

A well-written Visual letter. But suppose I am not a Visual? What are the chances of my reading any more of this letter? The answer: very slim.

Or consider the letter mentioned in the preceding chapter that reads, "(Our message) was **delivered** and **absorbed** by their clients...other messages were **designed** and **delivered** in the same effective way...I'd look forward to **walking** you through the entire program." (Emphasis is mine.)

This letter was written by someone who believes that the

best way to sell is to use kinesthetic metaphors. Unfortunately, this letter was sent to a Visual who ignored the message and, when asked about it a short time later, completely forgot ever having received the package.

Good letters that were sent to the wrong audience!

The problem with these letters is common and simple: they are written with a single language preference to an unknown audience. If you are going to write a Visual letter, it is wise to know that you are sending it to a Visual audience. Otherwise, you are wasting your time and money. Anticipate a mixed audience and use a language mix of all the preferences.

USE A VAK MIX

It is often useful to mix V, A, and K words in a single message. This is especially true in the following situations:

1. You do not know the language preference of your audience.

2. You want to use all three languages to increase the impact on your audience.

3. You want to avoid patterns of resistance.

• Unknown Audience

Often you must send a letter or speak to someone without knowing his or her language preference. On other occasions, you may be trying to influence a bigger audience where language preferences are probably mixed throughout the group. In such situations, you need to use all three languages.

> *"I have some information for you to **look** at. We can **talk** about it briefly, and I will show you how it can **work** for you."*

73

President Reagan's quote at the beginning of the chapter is an example of why he was often called "the great communicator." His simple statement incorporated Visual, Auditory, and Kinesthetic words. He was not pacing a specific person's language. Instead, he was using all three languages to enhance his message and to ensure that he matched everyone who would hear him.

A second way to mix your language is to *REWORD* your message and send the same message in three languages. This is especially useful in asking questions.

> *"Do you **see** any problems here? Is there anything we need to **talk** over more? Are you **comfortable** with this?"*
>
> *"Remember, selling requires the skill to **read** your clients, **speak** their language and **sell** them as they want to be sold."*

How often do you ask a group a question and receive no response? Could it be your choice of words that blocks the response? Try using all three languages to ask the same question. People will only "hear" the phrase that fits for them. No one will notice your being redundant.

> *Does anyone see a problem here?*
> *Is there something we need to talk more about?*
> *How do you feel about this proposal?*

If you notice you are not getting the response you would like, try changing your words. Instead of *"Does anyone see a problem here?"*, change your words to *"Have you heard anything that may cause a problem?"* or *"Anything here make you uncomfortable?"* Notice that the first question was Visual and was changed to Auditory and then to Kinesthetic. You can safely use all three phrases without risk of your audience noticing the redundancy.

> **NOTE:**
>
> When you have only communicated with someone through letters, it is often unwise to guess at language preference from the letter content. People do not always write their own letters. Sometimes an assistant takes an idea and writes the letter. Also, some people have a "letter-writing" language that is digital or artificial. If you have only interacted with someone through written correspondence, use a mix of languages to send your message until you can get more information on your prospect or target audience.

• Mix to Increase Impact

Visual words stimulate the visual pathways of the brain. Similarly, Auditory and Kinesthetic words have a neurological impact on the listener or reader. Therefore, if you want to have the strongest effect with your message, you should mix your words and phrases.

Listen to the great orators of our history and see how they mix languages to deliver their messages:

> *"When we let freedom ring, when we let it ring from every village and every hamlet, from every state and every city, we will be able to speed up that day when all of God's children, black men and white men...., will be able to join hands and sing in the words of the old Negro spiritual, 'Free at last! Free at last! Thank God Almighty, we are*

free at last!'" (Martin Luther King, Jr., "I Have a Dream", August 28, 1963.

"No man thinks more highly than I do of the patriotism...of the very worthy gentlemen who have just addressed the House. But different men often see the same subject in different lights...I shall speak forth my sentiments freely and without reserve...The war is actually begun! The next gale that sweeps from the north will bring to our ears the clash of resounding arms!...I know not what course others may take; but as for me, give me liberty, or give me death." (Patrick Henry, March 23, 1775.)

Great speakers have always known this secret: words can *energize* an audience. The right words create energy. When you mix your verbs and predicates to reflect Visual, Auditory, and Kinesthetic preferences, you are creating non-conscious mental activity in your audience. Mix your languages to generate the greatest possible impact from your words.

NOTE:

When writing a letter, even if you know the person's language preference, try to use a VAK mix as early in the letter as possible. This increases the likelihood of the letter being read immediately and with interest. Use the person's preferred language in the main body of the letter, but begin and end the letter with a VAK mix. The mix stimulates interest and neural activity, while the pacing builds rapport!

Just as people have a preferred language, they also tend to have a repertoire of responses and objections using their preferred language. One way to avoid those objections is to break the pattern and *avoid* their preferred language! Pace their initial word choice to build rapport and then lead them to a different language to bypass resistance.

For instance, people who live in the Visual world have a repertoire of Visual objections to what you are selling. They can react quickly to your attempts to close a sale or lead them, even though they may be comfortable with you as a person. Because they are so accustomed to having a "canned" response, they often deliver it without thinking.

"We are not **looking** at proposals at this time." (V)

"You really need to **talk** to purchasing about that." (A)

"I'm awfully **busy** and can't **take** the time right now." (K)

To avoid this kind of knee-jerk (conditioned) response or *pattern*, pace the initial language preference and then quickly lead the person to another language, one where there will be fewer con-ditioned responses.

> "I **see**. Can we **talk** for a moment, though?" (V-K)
>
> "I will be glad to **talk** with purchasing. You may be **excited** to see that...." (A-K)
>
> "Because you are **busy**, I want to **tell** you very quickly about what I can **show** you later..." (K-A-V)

As you move into a non-preferred language, you can guide a prospect away from his/her rehearsed responses. In this way, the prospect is more likely to actually notice what you are presenting, because you have gone outside their typical boundaries of perception, beyond what they expect to hear or see or feel.

Remember: you must first pace the person. But if you get an immediate objection, pace again and then lead into a new language.

NOTE:

Once you have moved past the objection, try to return to the person's preferred language as quickly as you can. A return to a mix is useful as you talk about features and benefits to help increase your impact on your listener. Then try to close by pacing the prospect's preferred language as much as possible. Don't stay out of sync too long.

EXERCISE

VAK Mixing

Add to each phrase two additional phrases to create a VAK mix.

1. Does this sound right?

2. Where do we need to look next?

3. Does this feel like the right direction to pursue?

VAK Mix EXERCISE: (Sample answers)

1. Does this sound right? *Does it look OK? Anything not fit right?*

2. Where do we need to look next? *What are the next issues we need to speak to? What is the next stone to turn over?*

3. Does this feel like the right direction to pursue? *Are there areas we need to talk more about? Does the map seem clear?*

EXERCISE

VAK Mixing #2

Write a brief memo or statement to express the following ideas using all three languages.

1. Our department needs to put quality first.

2. I want sales and production to work together in a cooperative manner.

3. I regret you have had a complaint about our product.

(Examples on next page)

VAK Mixing #2 Exercise: *Sample Answers*

1. Our department needs to put quality first.

> *I want to **see** quality **shouted** out throughout this department. Everything we **do** needs to **announce** that Quality comes first. We mean it, and our work **shows** it.* (V, A, K, A, K/V)

2. I want sales and production to work together in a cooperative manner.

> *Sales and production seem to often **line up** on opposite sides of issues. I want to **see** this change. **Talk** together to **solve** problems not just **highlight** the other guy's mistakes. (K, V, A, K, V)*

3. I regret you have had a complaint about our product.

> *I'm sorry to **hear** you have had a problem. Let me **see** what I **can do** right now to **solve** the problem. I'll **call** you back within the hour.* (A, V, K, K, A)

NOTE:

Use short words that are clearly Visual, Auditory, or Kinesthetic. For instance, use "see", "hear", "look at", or "get a feel for" rather than "examine", "investigate", "clear", or similar words that are either too long or could be coded as more than one possible language. (Is "clear" a K, A, or V word? Your answer probably depends on your own language preference!) Keep it simple.

EXERCISE

VAK Mixing #3

Rewrite the following "Business-like" phrases. Use a VAK mix.

1. Pursuant to your inquiry, I am forwarding some materials about our services. We have a reputation for quality and effectiveness. We are confident that we can meet your needs.

2. My colleagues and I would like the opportunity to explore with you how we can meet your needs and improve the functionality of your current systems.

3. I am taking this opportunity to introduce myself and the services of the AJAX COMPANY. We are a full-service organization dedicated to providing the most cost-efficient answer to your problems. Please let us know if you have any questions.

(Examples on next page)

VAK Mixing #3 Exercise: *Sample Answers*

1. Pursuant to your inquiry, I am forwarding some materials about our services. We have a reputation for quality and effectiveness. We are confident that we can meet your needs.

> *Thank you for your **call**. I have **sent** you some material to **look at** to introduce us. You may have **heard** about our reputation for quality, and we are **pleased** to **show** you how we can help you.* (A, K, V, A, K, K/V)

2. My colleagues and I would like the opportunity to explore with you how we can meet your needs and improve the functionality of your current systems.

> *I **look** forward to a chance to **talk** with you about your current systems. We want a short time to **tell** our story and to **see** if we can **help** you.* (V, A, A, V, K)

3. I am taking this opportunity to introduce myself and the services of the AJAX COMPANY. We are a full-service organization dedicated to providing the most cost-efficient answer to your problems. Please let us know if you have any questions.

> *I want you to **get to know** me and my company, the AJAX Company. As I **tell** you a little about us, I think you will **see** that we can **help** you and **help** you in a cost-efficient way. Let's **talk** a little and **see** what kind of questions we can **come up** with.* (K/D, A, V, K, K, A, V, K)

EXERCISE

VAK Mixing #4

Describe your business or product in three to four sentences. Include a full mix of V, A, and K words as early and as frequently as possible:

Example:
Lakin Associates is a group of psychologists who **help solve** people problems in organizations. **(K)** We interview candidates for key positions and **talk** to managers about problem employees or teams. **(A)** We help managers **look** at old problems in new ways. **(V)** We also **teach** skills and insights to help individuals or teams **work** more effectively, whether their job is selling, managing, or supervising. **(K)**

EXERCISE

Breaking the Pattern

Pace the response and then lead the person to a new language.

1. I can't see you right now.

2. This isn't a good time. Call back later.

3. I don't do business like this.

BREAKING THE PATTERN: Examples of possible responses:

1. I can't see you right now.
> *"Before we look for a better time, I want to just say..."*

2. This isn't a good time. Call back later.
> *"Great. When we talk then, I want to be able to help you see..."*

3. I don't do business like this.
> *"It can be hard. Let me quickly tell you the advantages..."*

7 *Using Eye Cues*

INTRODUCTION

As you have seen, language preferences can be identified by listening carefully to the words someone uses. The same neurological processes that govern language choice can also be observed when a person is only mentally forming words; that is, *thinking!*

There are often times when a prospect is thinking and not speaking or sharing those thoughts with you. You may lack rapport and the person is reluctant to tell you what you want to know. This frequently happens in interviews or initial cold calls. On other occasions, someone may not be able to verbalize his/her own thoughts. There are also occasions when a client is trying to hide thoughts from you. For instance, "price" may be the verbalized answer to how he selects a product, when in fact there is another issue driving the decision—an issue he does not choose to tell you.

Recognizing language preference in non-verbalized thinking can help you coax verbal behavior and influence action. The mental process of thinking is the same as if the person were verbalizing or acting, but it is non-verbal and sometimes non-conscious.

Wouldn't it be helpful to know the language in which that person is thinking? Wouldn't it be helpful to be able to phrase a question to match how a person is thinking, even before he/she speaks?

During the early NLP development, the researchers made a remarkable discovery. They noticed that when a person was thinking visual thoughts, the eyes would reveal this process. And when a person was thinking auditory thoughts, the eyes were in a position different from the visual thinker. By learning what to notice, you can identify language preferences without words being spoken. You can even notice when the words spoken and the thoughts preceding the words are inconsistent. With that information, you can use your questions and responses to build rapport and to lead the prospect to share more information.

Learning to notice language preference when a person is thinking is NOT an easy skill. It requires practice. But when you decide to learn and use it, you will discover that it can be one of the most powerful applications of NLP and The Unfair Advantage.

On the next pages, you will find a graphic "map" for identifying language preferences revealed by the eyes! The remainder of this chapter will initially explain how to use the Eye Map for identifying language preference in thought. The chapter will conclude with ideas for using this skill in interviewing and selling.

GUIDE TO INTERPRETING EYE CUES

The first step in learning to interpret eye cues is to learn the **Rows**. Ignore the difference between right or left. Since Row 3 is a more complex signal, begin by learning to notice "up" and "down" movements only (Row 1 and 2). If you can begin to recognize visual and auditory language in a person's thinking, you will have a powerful advantage without worrying about the finer distinction of left and right movement.

• **Learn the Rows First**

ROW 1 is the **Visual Row**. When a person's eyes are "looking" up, the person is thinking in the visual language. ("Looking" is put in quotes, because the individual is not actually looking at anything. Instead, he/she is accessing internal information. However, the eyes appear to be looking somewhere—in this case, up.) Sometimes individuals will also stare straight ahead, as if focusing about three feet in front of them. This is also a sign of Visual thinking.

ROW 2 is the **Auditory Row**. When a person appears to be "looking" into one of his/her ears, you know the person is thinking in the auditory language.

NOTE:

The interpretation of the Eye Map is based on the assumption of right-handedness. Many left-handed people DO NOT match this map. Depending on the degree of "left-handedness", some reverse the top row, some reverse the middle row, some reverse everything, and some reverse nothing. If you are talking with a left-handed person, you will have to observe eye movements in response to easy questions that do not invite resistance. As you begin to notice where the eyes go when remembering or when constructing, you will be able to calibrate the map to the person. Over time, this will become second-nature to you, but it is initially confusing. Be patient and practice.

WATCH THE EYES

CONSTRUCTED IMAGES

REMEMBERED IMAGES

PUTTING SOMETHING INTO WORDS

REMEMBERED AUDITORY

KINESTHETIC
(Body Sensations)

INTERNAL DIALOGUE

Reversed for me, I think...

89

ROW 3 is a mixed row. When a person "looks" down to <u>your</u> left, that (right-handed) person is thinking in a kinesthetic language. He/she may be feeling an internal feeling or experiencing (thinking about) a physical sensation. When a person "looks" down to <u>your</u> right, that person is talking to himself/herself. In a sense, this is another auditory language cue.

As you get more comfortable with recognizing eye cues, you can begin to make a finer distinction between up, down, left, and right.

NOTE:

Perhaps the most difficult aspect of learning this skill is the fact that eye movement is very fast. People will not stay in a position long enough for you to grab your EYE CODE sheet and look it up. Therefore, you must practice. The easiest and safest place to practice is with the television. Shows like <u>Leeza</u>, <u>20/20</u>, <u>Dateline</u>, <u>Oprah</u>, <u>Charlie Rose</u>, and others that interview non-actors can provide a rich opportunity for practicing hearing words *and* eye reading. It is important to find interviewers who ask unexpected questions that force the person to actually think. Otherwise, no thought is necessary to respond and no neural activity is involved. The eyes give cues only if there is a real thought process occurring.

• Begin to Notice Right and Left Direction

ROW 1, the visual row, can be divided into "remembered"--upper right (your right) and "constructed"--upper left. "Remembered" means the person is mentally picturing something he/she has actually seen. "Constructed" means the person is mentally picturing something that has not actually been seen but is or has been imagined.

For instance, if a right-handed person is remembering something specific that was seen in a proposal, the eyes will go up and to your right. If the person is thinking about what was NOT in the proposal and in his opinion should have been, the eyes will go up and to your left.

NOTE:

Learning to recognize the six eye cues is difficult. Some people barely move their eyes. Others often use exaggerated eye movements as part of their pattern of expressions. Also, some people blink when their eyes move and the movement actually takes place beneath the eyelid. That movement can still cue you about the language preference, but it is hard for most people to see.

You have to learn to calibrate when the eyes are actually giving you a cue. This process becomes automatic with practice, but it can be daunting in the early learning stages. Be persistent and practice. The power of using this information will reward you well for your effort!

In ROW 2, the auditory row, if the same person appears to be looking into the ear on your right, that individual is hearing something actually heard, such as something someone else may have said or a sound or song that can be recalled. If the person appears to be looking into the ear on your left, the individual is constructing a sound, such as putting an idea into words or hearing an imaginary sound.

For instance, if a person is asked to report on what someone said and the eyes go to your left, the individual may be trying to summarize or paraphrase what they heard. If the eyes go to your right, they may be reporting verbatim the words of another.

In ROW 3, if a right-handed person is looking down to your right, an "internal dialogue" is taking place. Frequently, the head will tilt a bit to your right when this occurs. Even though it is internal, the person is still talking. Therefore, eyes down to your right are a cue that the person is in an auditory mode. A question such as "*What do you say to yourself when...*" can often get the individual to say aloud what was being thought silently!

If the eyes are looking down to your left, the same individual is in a kinesthetic mode. The kinesthetic feeling may be internal ("*I am worried about that*") or external ("*This seat is getting uncomfortable*").

USE EYE CUES IN INTERVIEWING

People often resist answering a direct question in an interview, whether it is a sales interview or an employment interview. However, the resistance often comes AFTER the person has thought about the answer. In other words, the resistance is to telling you what was thought. By reading the thinking process, you at least will know the language the other person is using, and you can use your words to help reduce the resistance.

The eyes reveal language preference AT THAT MOMENT. Therefore, there are three key times to *notice* the eyes:

1. Immediately after you have asked a question.

2. During a pause, when the person is searching for a thought.

3. Immediately before a person speaks.

With observation, timing, and skillful wording of questions, you can help people tell you what you need to know.

> *I was asked to interview a young man as a preparation to his being fired. I knew he would not be forthcoming with me, because he viewed me as a threat. I had worked with his company management nearly ten years and had a close relationship with his superiors.*
>
> *I began the interview with a digital question, knowing I would phrase my next question based on either his eye movements or his words, and I did not want to be misled by his inadvertently matching my language choice.*
>
> *"Ned, we need to explore the last few years a bit."*
>
> *His eyes went up and to my right as he said with complete apathy, "OK."*
>
> *Encouraged by this out-pouring of emotion, I continued, using the only cue I had been given--his eye movement.*
>
> *"How have you seen the last year?"*
>
> *Again, his eyes went up and to my right. "OK, I guess."*
>
> *"Ned, how do you think others have seen your performance?" I asked quickly, trying to get my question out while he was still visualizing.*
>
> *Within a few minutes, he was describing the nightmare he had been living. He knew he was unable*

to do his job, and for the last year he had avoided finishing assignments knowing that others would pick up the task and take the blame if something failed. He had been hiding for a year in fear of being discovered. He lamented, "I know if people saw how poorly I have been doing my job, I would be fired."

NOTE:

In order for the eyes to give you clues, the person must actually be thinking about your question. If a question is too obvious or a person is so well prepared that thinking is not required to provide a comment, the eyes will not move. (Watch a politician give "sound bites" to the media.)

Consequently, two things are needed. First, you need rapport to encourage the person to think about what you ask. Second, the questions must be difficult and complex enough to prevent sound bites. If you think you are getting a canned answer OR if you notice the eyes do not move prior to the answer, try expanding the question to make it more difficult to answer. Also, if an answer is too general, insist on specifics. *(What was the person's name? Who suggested the price ceiling? Can you think of at least one time when an exception was made?)* Usually the necessity to access memory in responding to the more difficult question will lead to useable eye cues.

An interview that began with no interaction and painful distrust ended with rich information and someone ready to hear the bad news. The secret? The careful phrasing of questions to match his thinking process.

USE EYE CUES TO UNLOCK A RESPONSE

A quick and timely question to match the thinking process can often unlock a response that was being held back. If you can intervene at just the right time with the right question, the non-conscious mind does not screen the response. By matching the language of the thinking process, people will experience the sensation of talking to themselves rather than talking to you. There is even some evidence to suggest that when this quick intervention into the thinking process occurs, the respondent may not even be aware of having spoken the answer aloud!

> *A management consultant was about to close on a project for the State of Illinois. He traveled to Springfield to meet with the person who had been coordinating the proposal requests.*
>
> *On arrival, he discovered the coordinator had been replaced by two cocky young men who took great delight in staring at each other in a knowing manner whenever asked a question.*
>
> *To make matters worse, the key specifications of the proposal had been changed!*
>
> *"These aren't the specs I have been working with," lamented the consultant. The two state employees smiled, looked at one another in their knowing way, and said nothing.*
>
> *"Where did they come from?" the consultant asked. Again, no response, but he noticed both men moved their eyes right.*

95

Without a second's hesitation, he added, "Who told you these numbers?" Instantly, one of the men blurted out a name— a name, it turned out, who was the principle behind the project yet had not been identified.

The consultant thanked them and proceeded to contact the primary project manager, ultimately getting the assignment.

The state employees in the above situation had no intention of revealing the name of their boss. However, by quickly matching the language of the question to the eye movement, the consultant was able to get a response.

USE EYE CUES TO GET PAST NONCONSCIOUS ROADBLOCKS

Sometimes people are not forthcoming with information because they are not aware of their own thought process. It is not always due to resistance. They may not be trying to hide infor-mation from you. They may simply have nonconscious roadblocks that are getting in the way of their own awareness or insight. Typically, you will notice the person saying one thing, such as, "*It does not bother me*", while the eyes are indicating a Kinesthetic feeling response. When this occurs, the internal state, revealed by the eye cue, is probably the more influential force on any important decision. Use that information to guide your use of words.

A departmental director from a midwestern hospital was charged with recommending a new million-dollar com-munication system for her hospital.

Two major competitors surfaced. They sent a small army of engineers and technicians to teach the director how to understand the complex features and benefits of what their particular company had to offer.

I asked her, "How are you going to choose?"

Moving her eyes up and to my right, she replied, "I am going to carefully read all the material they provide and find the one that can do the best job for us."

A congruent and a sincere answer. However, I knew she had no intention of becoming a systems expert. She would hire such a person. Computer technology was of no interest to her.

So I asked her, "After reading all that, how are you going to make the decision to recommend one over the other?"

Her eyes went down and to my left as she said, "I plan to carefully study the features and benefits of each and choose the best one."

Her eyes told me the real formula for her "BUY" decision. She would make the final decision based on emotional (kinesthetic) factors. And she did not know it! She was acting as if her decision would be rational and logical.

I then asked, "What will it take for you to _feel_ better about one than the other?" (a kinesthetic question).

She said, "I need to know that if the system crashes, I will have inside communication in 30 seconds and a backup outside line in about 45 seconds." Both vendors could probably meet those criteria.

"Also," she added, "I don't really want Vendor A. But they installed $150,000 in wiring last *year in anticipation of winning this contract. If I recommend Vendor B, my boss will have to ask the finance committee for an additional $150,000 to pay Vendor A and this will embarrass him. I need to find a resolution that will not embarrass my boss."*

The eyes had told me the buying formula. Knowing that formula, I could ask the right questions to discover the real issues.

NOTE:

When a person talks to you, the eyes will often move just before he/she speaks or just after you ask a question. This is your cue. As the person searches for words or talks internally, the eyes are telling you the language being used. Use that information to guide your questions. Ask questions that can help build rapport and get valuable information. Also, do not be afraid to jump in with a follow-up question using the eye cue data BEFORE the person actually responds. This is often a useful technique for getting someone to say something that might otherwise have been held back.

Eye cues give you access to how a person is thinking. When used well, it can give you amazing power to open conversations and influence an individual. It is difficult to master the skill, but even if you can only use it occasionally, it is worth the effort.

One final thought: You cannot conduct a normal conversation and stare at someone's eyes. It does not help establish rapport! Reading eye cues is what you do when the conversation is NOT flowing–when someone is thinking and not talking. Once the conversation is going well and you are getting the information you need, you do not need to worry about the eyes. Use the eyes as a tool to help you move toward rapport, openness, clarity, and congruety when such results are not occurring. It can be a powerful tool in your repertoire.

NOTE:

DO NOT try to use eye cues to determine if a person is lying. You will never get good enough at noticing, at asking just the right question, or at timing the question to safely determine if a person is fabricating an answer. You will be misled and embarrassed more often than you will be right. Use the cues to help you influence and sell more efficiently and effectively, not to be a policeman.

EXERCISE

Eye Cues

What would you say under the following circumstances?

1. One of your customers says to you, *"I've got a real problem with your last delivery."* Just PRIOR to his saying that, his eyes went up and to <u>your</u> left. What would you say?

Horizontal and to <u>your</u> right...?

2. A customer says, *"I'm real upset about your service."* Just PRIOR to her saying this, her eyes go down and to <u>your</u> left. What would you say?

Up and to <u>your</u> right...?

3. A key prospect says, *"You've got some tough competition on this one."*
Just PRIOR to saying this, his eyes go up and to <u>your</u> right. What would you say?

Down and to <u>your</u> right...?

Eye Cues Exercise: *Sample Answers*

What would you say under the following circumstances?

1. One of your customers says to you, *"I've got a real problem with your last delivery."* Just PRIOR to his saying that, his eyes went up and to your left. What would you say?

> A: *"What would you have liked to have seen different?"* (The customer was seeing something in his head. You need to find this out to meet his expectations in the future.)

Horizontal and to your right...?

> A: *"I haven't heard a thing. What happened? Did someone say something went wrong?"*
> (The customer is recalling something specific that was heard. He may have heard about a problem or someone may have told him to do something about it. For instance, there may have been something broken in the shipment, and he is recalling the sound of the package being delivered, for instance. Whatever the case, he is recalling specific words or sounds.)

2. A customer says, *"I'm real upset about your service."* Just PRIOR to her saying this, her eyes go down and to your left. What would you say?

> A: *"I'm sorry you are upset. Let's do something about it right now. What can I do to solve this problem?"*
> (Kinesthetic emphasis.)

Up and to <u>your</u> right...?

> A: *"I'm sorry. Let's look at what was wrong and I'll take care of it. What specifically did you see that was not up to your expectations?"*
> (The customer was picturing something specific. You need to focus on that.)

3. A key prospect says, *"You've got some tough competition on this one."*
Just PRIOR to saying this, his eyes go up and to <u>your</u> right. What would you say?

> A: *"You have seen our proposal. Where specifically do you see the toughest problem?*

Down and to <u>your</u> right...?

> A: *"What does your intuition tell you will be our biggest problem?*

8 *Buying Patterns*

"The difference between the right word and the almost right word is the difference between lightning and a lightning bug." —Mark Twain

DISCOVER THE BUYING FORMULA

People usually have good explanations for why they buy something.

"The db separation is nearly 10% better than the one I have now!"

"The accessing speed of the hard drive is a full 2 micro-seconds faster!"

"I am making an important presentation tomorrow and I need the confidence this new outfit gives me."

"This firm has been auditing corporations in our industry for fifty years and can provide the perspective we need."

"I bought this stock today, because the trend line is definitely indicating a correction is coming and I think it will perform well in such times."

"For the first time, his proposal really made
sense and was not just pie-in-the-sky projections."

We all have great reasons for buying products, services, or ideas. The only problem: those reasons usually come *after* we have decided to buy.

The real thinking process that determines if a person buys a product or service tends to be non-conscious. And habitual. The process will usually not change over time. The rationalization and intellectualizing get better, but the fundamental process stays largely unchanged for that person for that specific product or service.

If John bought a house once, he will buy his next house the same way. Sure, he will be more sophisticated, ask better questions, or analyze more completely the details. But the actual "buy" decision will follow the exact same strategy as before.

This does not mean John will buy a car the same way he bought the house. He may buy a computer system or a consulting project in a completely different way from how he bought the house. But if he bought a consulting project last year, he will buy the next one the same way.

Therefore, **if you want to know how to sell something, find out how the person bought it the last time**. A formula exists, and with close attention to language preferences, you can discover the formula.

The key to the formula is to notice the language preference when answering "*What about (the house) resulted in your deciding to buy it?*" Notice that the question is digital. You want the answer to come from the other person without a risk that he/she may be mirroring you. If the response is, "*It was beautiful*", then the first part of the buying formula is Visual. "*It was beautiful and I fell in love with it*" gives you two parts of the formula. The Visual element led to the Kinesthetic decision to buy. While the person is probably a Kinesthetic individual, the buying formula tells you what triggers the Kinesthetic reaction. In this case, it was a Visual stimulus.

Typically, people will not tell you the real reasons for a decision. They may not know. The real reasons may be non-conscious. At such times, it is useful to use the eyes as the cue to the buying pattern rather than the words. This is especially important if you notice an incongruency between what is said and the eyes. For instance, if someone says, "*I liked the way it looked*", yet the eyes moved into a Kinesthetic pattern, code the buying cue as a K or feeling cue rather than a Visual cue from the word "look". The key to selling with a person's buying strategy is to learn the language preference formula the person has used in the past. The more parts of the process you can learn, the stronger will be the impact of your selling. Then, "play back" the formula two or three times as you describe what you want to sell, using the person's language formula to guide your choice of words.

> *I was having breakfast with a regional manager of a national service organization and learned he was planning to buy a house. He was interested in The Unfair Advantage, and I decided to use his interest in houses to demonstrate one of the techniques.*
>
> *I first asked, "John, you have bought a house before, right?"*
>
> *"Oh, yes. The last one was several years ago, however."*
>
> *Since time makes no difference, I asked him, "Think about that last house you bought. (Notice the digital choice of words. I did not want to take a chance on John pacing me!) What was the first thing that made you decide to buy that house?"*

His eyes went up and to my right and he replied,
"I liked its location and the way it looked." (V)

"What was the second thing about the house
that made you want to buy it?" I asked.

He quickly said "Price." More important to
me was the fact that his eyes moved down and to
my left. (K)

Again, I asked, "What was the third thing that
made you want to buy that house?"

"The interest rates were low then." His eyes
went up and to my right. (V)

I looked at him a moment and said, "John, I
saw a house the other day, a nice well-built home
that you might want to look at. (VKV) I think it
is quite attractive, and I've got a feeling that you
will like what you see. (VKV) I don't know if it
shows well, but the builder has a solid reputation,
and you may want to see this place." (VKV)

He immediately suggested we leave breakfast
for another day and go right now to see this house.
Needless to say, he was very disappointed to learn
I was making up the whole story. I knew of no
such house. But if I did, I knew how he wanted
to buy it! I sold him exactly how he wanted to be
sold---VKV.

With John, in the story above, his formula was V-K-V. His
first decision point was the result of a Visual process. We do not
know what he actually saw, because his words did not match
his eyes. But we know that something Visual sold him, possibly his own visualization of his family in the house. Because
our rapport was strong, I was able to probe until I found three

parts of his formula. Naturally, the decision to buy can be more complex than this, but three parts of the formula are usually sufficient to be effective in the playback. If the circumstances had been different, I might have settled for only two parts. One helps, but two give me a stronger advantage.

The buying formula for a specific product or service is not likely to change over time. However, the formula for one product does not necessarily transfer to another. For instance, the formula a person uses to buy a car would not necessarily be the same formula he/she uses to buy a management consultant, accept a stock recommendation, or use to pick a house.

People often like to talk about their past. Therefore, it is usually easy to get them to tell you what they did last time. You can ask, *"What made you decide to buy your last one?"* and you can learn a lot about the buying strategy. You can also use a variation such as, *"Why are you needing a new portfolio manager? What was the first thing that made you decide to part with the last one?"* Accepting and rejecting are usually based on the same criteria. Remember to ask your questions as digitally as possible. The answers to these questions can help you identify what is important to the other person. By listening carefully to the words and watching the eyes, you can also begin to identify the language formula that the person uses for buying.

The objective in discovering the buying formula is to identify the priorities in the person's thinking for accepting (or rejecting) what you are selling, and then use that information to sell your proposal.

Market research helps companies identify what their customers want in terms of products or features. Would it not be helpful if market research could determine if there exists a "typical" buying formula for a product or service? While we doubt such simplicity exists, it would be worth exploring.

Until then, it remains a good practice to write marketing materials or general-release publications using a rich mix of visual, auditory, and kinesthetic words to ensure that you are appealing to at least the first step in every person's buying formula somewhere in the key areas of your document.

One final comment: Because this skill enables you to be extremely persuasive, your integrity is critical in ensuring that what you are selling is indeed needed and beneficial to the other person.

NOTE:

You can sell by presenting your product or service in the order dictated by the buying formula of your prospects. However, you should also be prepared to provide ample supporting information and logical reasons to help them build their own conscious rationale for buying. Do this *after* **you have psychologically sold them.**

"*You know, you are going to feel good about this decision, because.....***" They need to mentally rehearse answering this question to prevent buyer's remorse and to help them respond to questions from others.**

EXERCISE

Buying Patterns

You have asked questions and determined your prospect buys cars using a K-A-K strategy. Describe the car you want to sell them.

Convince your manager to recommend your proposal to her boss. You know she uses a A-K-A buying process to "buy" proposals.

Describe *your* product or service to someone with a V-A-K buying formula.

Buying Patterns Exercise: *Sample Answers*

You have asked questions and determined your prospect buys cars using a K-A-K strategy. Describe the car you want to sell them.

> *"I have a feeling you may have heard about our hottest seller. You drive it, then we'll talk about it a while before we move to another one, if necessary. I love this car...I can't wait to hear what your feelings are after driving it."*

Convince your manager to recommend your proposal to her boss. You know she uses an A-K-A buying process to "buy" proposals.

> *"I hear you want to talk to George about the proposal. Can I tell you some hard selling points that might help him hear the advantages quickly and succinctly? If we tell him up front the solid basis for the plan, I think he will say "go". I've heard a lot of people are excited by the plan, and I'd like to tell you their feedback."*

Describe *your* product or service to someone with a V-A-K buying formula.

> *What does it look like? What can people see? Picture this...?*
>
> *What are people saying about it? Is there a sound associated with it? Do you listen to your customers?*
>
> *How do people feel? Is there a touch or quality to the product that is important?*
>
> *Does it excite or warm or move people?*
>
> *"When you see what others have said about us, you'll gain a better appreciation for what we do."*
>
> *"When you look at what we have done over the past twenty years, you will hear our pride in the way we help people grow."*

9 *Non-Verbal Mirroring*

"For it is mutual trust, even more than mutual interest, that holds human associations together." —H.L. Mencken

INTRODUCTION

So far in this workbook, you have learned to pace and lead through the use of your words. You can also pace—quickly and effectively—without saying a word. Instead of matching language preferences, you can gain rapport and trust by matching posture or physical movements. The process is often called "mirroring." It is the fastest and easiest way to gain rapport with another person or with a group. But it also carries a risk of being obvious, and therefore, ineffective. Learn the process and then practice being subtle in the execution.

NOTICE "NATURAL MIRRORING

Mirroring is a natural occurrence between people who already know each other and feel comfortable with one another. The next time you go to a party or visit a restaurant, look around. Notice the people around you. Can you tell who is in rapport and who is not? If you notice carefully, you will see or hear a similarity between two people in rapport. The body posture of one mirrors the other. If you were able to listen to the conversation, you might even notice the vocal tempo and loudness of one is matched by the other. If a couple in rapport is eating at a table, you may notice that they are eating at the same pace and, perhaps, taking a sip from their drinks at the same time.

At a company meeting, notice the postures of the people. You can often tell who is in agreement with whom. When someone is speaking, those who are most likely to agree with what is being said are most likely to be mirroring the speaker!

This phenomenon, physical mirroring, is easily observed. The opposite occurrence, physical mismatching, is also common. What happens when you are approached by a panhandler? Have you ever sat on a bench in a park or a bus and had someone join you on that bench that you did not wish to "encourage" with your attention? What did you do? You probably physically mismatched the person, leaning a different direction, crossing your legs in the opposite way, or looking a different direction.

Physical mirroring—and non-mirroring—is a natural reaction to another person. In most cases, it happens automatically, and you never notice it. The unfair advantage occurs when you *purposefully* use it to create rapport. Once you have established rapport, you can forget the process until it is needed again.

> *The President of an import business was making a proposal to a prospect. Although he had prepared for several days, the anxiety of the moment left him with a blank mind. He forgot what he had planned to say.*
>
> *Even though he had only experienced a brief introduction to NLP, he called upon his skill to*

physically mirror his customer. He mirrored the prospect as he talked about his company. Soon he became more comfortable as he noticed the prospect being more relaxed with him.

He reported back that never in his life had he experienced such a success. In about an hour, the prospect indicated his readiness to sign the contract, and price had not even been negotiated! The result: a $5 million dollar contract.

CREATE RAPPORT WITH PHYSICAL MIRRORING

When you mirror the posture of someone, that person begins to feel more comfortable with you and pay more attention to what you are saying. The key is to mirror as much of the other person's posture as possible. There are two caveats, however:

1. Don't make yourself uncomfortable.

2. Don't get noticed.

Physical mirroring makes a strong non-conscious connection between you and the other person. If you are physically uncomfortable, the other person will sense your discomfort, internalize that discomfort and feel uncomfortable with you! The irony is that *your* discomfort causes the other person to lose rapport with you.

You will also lose rapport if you are noticed using this skill. The other person will feel you are mimicking him or her. You will be seen as manipulative and rapport will be impossible to recover. Mirroring is the fastest way to gain rapport, but it can also cost you a relationship if used poorly.

Avoid being noticed by delaying your positioning; that is, if the other person leans right, wait until he/she is speaking or otherwise distracted from watching you before you lean in the same direction. If the person then suddenly leans forward, again wait for several seconds before reacting.

For instance, suppose you and your prospect are both sitting back and the other person suddenly leans forward. You cannot immediately react. Instead, you can turn in your chair or cross your legs. Then ask a question to distract attention away from you. As the other person begins to respond, you can display your interest in the answer by leaning forward a little bit. Increase the lean as you talk until you are mirroring again.

You do not have to mirror the whole posture of another person. You can mirror as little as the head. You can also mirror gestures as long as they are subtle. The more aspects of the person you can mirror, however, the more powerful the results. Always give yourself a little delay between noticing a posture and mirroring it. This delay can keep you from having your technique noticed.

> *The President of an architectural engineering firm was attending a dinner sponsored by the municipality that had requested proposals for a building project. Also attending the dinner were his key competitors.*
>
> *During cocktails, he systematically mirrored each of the key members of the city's committee. Then all were seated for dinner, and he continued to mirror the the head and shoulder posture of the key decision makers, one at a time, of course.*
>
> *Within a few minutes he was startled with two observations. First, he noticed that the three key decision makers were all mirroring him--lifting their glasses together and eating at the same pace.*

*Even more amazing, he became aware that the
only person to whom they were directing questions
or comments was HIM! He reported having the
sensation that all the competition in the room
seemed to fade into the background, visually as well
as auditorially. And the committee members were
behaving as though they had the same perception!*

MIRROR TO TEST RAPPORT

One of the powers of physical mirroring is reflected in the
preceding story. When you are in rapport with another person,
not only does that person feel comfortable with you, he or she
will actually mirror you without knowing it! Therefore, you
can test rapport by changing your posture to no longer mirror
the other person. If he/she then adjusts to *your* movement, you
have strong evidence of the rapport that exists.

In a discussion, for instance, you may want to decide if it
is time to tell your price or bring up a point that might cause
resistance. You can test the strength of your rapport with the
other person before you bring up the topic. Assuming you
have been mirroring his/her posture, change your posture . If
the rapport is strong, you will notice the other person suddenly
following you!

*I was having lunch with a prospect and had
been mirroring his posture off and on for about
an hour. When I was about to close the sale of a
project, I leaned forward and picked up my glass of
water. As I did so, I noticed my prospect following
my lead and picking up his glass.*

*I noticed something else, too. The waitress had
failed to fill his glass. As we talked and I sipped*

from my glass, he continued following my behavior, raising and lowering his glass, oblivious to the fact that it was empty!

One easy way to practice mirroring is to watch an interview program on television. Concentrate on one guest and pretend you are conducting the interview. Pretend to ask questions. While you do so, mirror the person's posture. Remember to wait a few seconds before you react to a change in posture or a new movement.

MIRROR A SMALL GROUP

Suppose you are presenting before a committee or a small group. How do you physically mirror and build rapport with several people?

One truism of public speaking is "look your audience in the eye." But why? What is accomplished by staring several seconds into the eyes of someone while you speak? It seems that such a rule only runs a risk of making both speaker and audience uncomfortable.

However, if eye contact includes mirroring of posture, it becomes a powerful rapport builder. Therefore, when you are presenting to a committee or small group, choose someone to look at (briefly), and mirror the SHOULDERS AND HEAD posture as you speak. Casually work around the group, subtly adjusting your head posture to match each person. Or out of the corner of your eye, focus on one or two key people and mirror them, even when talking to someone else in the room.

I was to present to a group of ten CEOs who were meeting in Northern Wisconsin. The chairman of the group, as a way of preparing me, warned me that one member was particularly cantankerous and often rude to guest speakers and I should not be offended if he left immediately upon the start of my presentation.

As luck would have it, this particular gentleman was scheduled to make a brief report prior to my being introduced. As he spoke, I politely listened to him while also casually glancing around the room, all the while mirroring his physical posture, including the way he was holding a pen.

When I was introduced and took my place at the front of the room, everyone was polite, but one pair of eyes was glued to me. This same person was the first person to volunteer a response to my questions and the most vocal participant in the exercises. The man who had been described to me as rude and cantakerous was my most enthusiastic audience member throughout the entire presentation!

NOTE:

During a small group presentation, people will ask questions or make comments that warrant a response from you. When this occurs, take one or two steps toward the person with the question. As you do so, mirror his or her head. You can also mirror arm or hand position as you begin to respond to the question.

MIRROR A LARGE GROUP

Suppose you are presenting in a large hall before 500 or more people. You certainly cannot mirror the heads and shoulders of such a crowd or you would soon hurt yourself. How do you physically mirror and build rapport with a large audience? Easy. You direct your audience to do something and you do it, too.

How do the pros do it? Almost every professional speaker uses a variant of the same set of behaviors, such as the following:

> *"How many have heard me before?"*
> (Speaker raises his/her hand to model the behavior.)
> *"Who would like to be thinner and healthier after today?"*
> *"Are there any people in the audience who would like to be richer?"*

What do these comments have in common? How are they similar to the Japanese practice of work teams doing calisthenics or singing the company song?

These are all examples of forced physical mirroring. The audience is now mirroring the "modeled" action of the speaker. You direct the audience to move and you mirror the same movement. Another way to mirror a large group is to direct their attention to a page in a handout or a line on the overhead slide. *"If everyone would turn to page 14 for a moment..."* and then pause while they (**and you**) turn pages and look at the page. A simple technique, yet it is an effective way to pull a group of people together and to build instant rapport with an audience.

Another technique accomplishes the same group rapport: jokes. If you can make a group laugh—and you laugh with them— you have strengthened rapport. Laughter is a form of physical movement and can be used to create the mirroring opportunity that leads to rapport.

Professional speakers everywhere tell jokes or make their audiences laugh. Zig Ziglar is a master persuasive speaker. In his excellent tapes on goals, he asks his audience, "Raise your hand if you have heard me before or if this is your first time." He gets physical movement <u>and</u> laughter, both of which he mirrors.

Audience response can also alert you that you may have lost rapport and need to do something. In one of his audio tapes, Ziglar tells a joke midway through his program. For some reason, few people laugh. He immediately stops his presentation and uses the hand-raising comment mentioned above. He instinctively knew he had lost his audience when he noticed no one laughed. Being a master speaker, he knew how to bring the audience back to him.

MIRROR THE VOICE

Posture is not the only kind of non-verbal mirroring. Speech tone, tempo, loudness, length of vocal phrases and even aspects of an accent are verbal behaviors that can be mirrored for rapport building.

Listen to a master sales professional on the phone. If you know his/her customers, you can probably identify which one is on the phone by noticing subtle changes in the voice of the sales professional.

I am always amazed by the number of top sales professionals who tell me that they have noticed themselves copying vocal characteristics of a customer on the phone and consciously tried to stop themselves. They fear they will be noticed and accused of mimicking. They have no reason to fear this. After all, who notices their own accent?

Hone this skill and increase your flexibility to mirror as many aspects of a customer's voice as possible. The more behaviors that can be mirrored, the stronger the rapport.

Physical and vocal mirroring are simple, easy-to-learn skills. They are powerful and rewarding when you want to create quick rapport. A little practice will help you develop smoothness and comfort with the skill.

The next time you are in a group of people, choose one person to mirror. Do not stare or make it obvious you are focusing on that individual. Simply mirror his/her behavior and notice how quickly the person will begin to give you more than casual attention.

NOTE:

Mirroring vocal behavior is an effective rapport builder. However, care must be taken not to be noticed AND not to have a third party notice. If you are presenting to a committee, for instance, it is risky to mirror the vocal characteristics of one person, then change when addressing a second person. A third person may notice what you are doing and you will lose rapport and credibility.

---

10 Creating Action With Words

"If you cry 'Forward!' you must without fail make plain in what direction to go. Don't you see that if, without doing so, you call out the word to both a monk and revolutionary, they will go in directions precisely opposite?"
—Anton Chekhov

WORDS CREATE ACTION

The mind is not passive. It responds to words, consciously and unconsciously. Words or sounds can effect you even when you are not aware you heard them.

Have you ever found yourself humming an irritating little tune that you cannot get out of your head yet you have no idea when you heard it? You probably did not consciously hear it, but your brain noticed it, maybe on the car radio this morning or on the television that your son was watching as you walked by, thinking of something else at the time. (Can we please forget the Barney song!)

The same is true for the written word. Perhaps you have skimmed a page in a newspaper and then discovered a phrase or idea is suddenly in your head. You do not recall reading it, but your mind somehow processed it as your eyes moved down the page.

Verbs or action words are especially powerful. They create mental action in those who hear or read them. There is some evidence that the brain has special areas that respond to verbs more quickly than to nouns, for instance. There are also strong arguments by Chomsky and others that the brain unconsciously searches for meaningful verb and object phrases as it processes language. It is looking for an action statement.

By using verbs or action words, you can create mental activity in another person. Such activity is very similar to the mental activity that occurs prior to a person's physical action or decision-making. Therefore, with the right words, you can create a *mental rehearsal* of what you want a person to do. This rehearsal familiarizes the brain with the action and increases the likelihood of the desired action taking place. Even if someone consciously resists your arguments, the person's mind cannot resist the impact you can have if you use the right words. (Remember *"Do not think of a pink elephant"?*)

Your own words create activity in your mind. Your mind wants to respond to your direction, even if you inadvertently tell it the wrong thing.

> *You are a golfer standing at the tee. You tell yourself "Don't hit it in the woods." What happens? Your ball flies into the woods. Your mind processed the statement, "hit it in the woods," and you did.*

You can use the power of your own words to motivate yourself. You can even use your own thoughts, when well-disciplined and carefully structured, to manage blood pressure, depression, asthma, stress, and scores of other physical maladies. The idea of using your own words to influence yourself is the broadest application of NLP today. It is the basis of much of the work of Tony Robbins or Brian Tracy as well as dozens of similar self-help programs.

But the power of "message engineering" is the discovery that you can use *your* words to influence how the *other person* thinks. If you want people to do something, you must lead them with your words. By carefully engineering your words, you can begin to lead your audience toward the outcome you want.

> *The President of a manufacturing company was invited to bid to offer his product on two pages of a national retailer's catalogue. The final phase of the bidding process was a formal presentation to the senior management of the catalog group. The key factor of the President's message was to impress the catalog group's management team with his company's ability to be a reliable and trustworthy partner, and he had little time to do it.*
>
> *The plan was to script a three-minute opening speech that would emphasize the message "Trust ABCo." During the opening comments, the phrase "trust ABCo." was repeated and paraphrased several times. Each time, however, the surrounding sentences masked or embedded the message to avoid attracting attention. (See Chapter 11 for ideas for embedding messages.)*
>
> *When the winning bid was announced, the president was dismayed to learn his company had come in third! The price differential had put him out of the running. A few months later, however, a call came from the retailer. The winning bidder was unable to produce as promised. The bidding*

*was to be reopened. "Normally," the president was told, "We would automatically offer the contract to the number two bidder. However, our team felt we could **trust ABCo.** and wanted to offer you a second chance."*

This time the outcome was different. The company was awarded a $5 million contract—the largest contract that year in the industry.

Was it a coincidence? Or was the "second chance" the direct result of careful use of words to influence the thinking of the audience?

The traditional selling concept of "trial closing" takes on a new context when you realize every statement you make can be a type of trial close. By using words to tell someone what you want, you are moving them toward your "close."

LEAD WITH ACTION STATEMENTS

If you want to influence someone, to get a person or a group to do as you want them to do, you must first tell them—tell them with clear, well-designed action statements.

Sometimes you send an action command without realizing it! A quick and simple lesson in linguistics. Consider the following phrases:

1. *"Johnny, stay on the porch."*
2. *"Johnny, don't get off the porch."*

These sentences appear to be sending the same message to Johnny. You would like Johnny to remain on the porch.

However, the brain does not interpret the messages that way. The brain unconsciously responds quickest to words that stimulate the nervous system, especially visual, auditory, or action/feeling (kinesthetic) words. It responds first to the action phrases. Therefore, the two sentences tell the brain two different things:

1. Stay on the porch
2. Get off the porch

What happened to the "don't" part of message number 2? It gets lost in the process. To process the phrase, the brain must first respond to the action. The mental rehearsal reflects the action statement. The brain must ignore the negative to respond to the linguistic structure of the sentence. Think about the following statements:

> *"Do not worry about the effect of this policy change."*
> *"When you contract with us, you do not have to ask if APEX will still be in business next year."*
> *"Stop trying to find a better deal."*
> *"Jill, do not hit your brother."*

In each case, these messages are likely to create the opposite effect than what was intended. Some advertisers spend millions of dollars to send the wrong message, as these examples from a few headlines in recent ads demonstrate:

> *"Ramada will pay you to **sleep with the competition**"*
>
> (Does Ramada really want us to sleep at Holiday Inn?)
>
> *"The Oldsmobile Edge. **Demand better.**"*
>
> (Are they suggesting I ask for a Rolls Royce?)
>
> Other advertisers just miss sending an action command:

"I can see you in an Eagle Talon."
(Wouldn't "See yourself in an Eagle Talon" be more of a direct action command?)
"Have you driven a Ford lately?"
(If not, drive a Ford today! Close, but no cigar.)
"If you are not using Diner's Club, you are missing the point."
(No action words.)

Tag lines and slogans in advertising are excellent examples of where action commands could be wisely used. *"Fly Delta"*, or *"Please don't squeeze the Charmin"* are all examples of action phrases using the product's name. However, lines such as *"Serving America's Needs", Rising"* or *"We are Beatrice"* influence no one.

HAVE A CLEAR OBJECTIVE

An action command must be clear. To be clear, you must know what you want to happen. Your objective must be clear. Do you want the person to...

...Buy your product/service?
...Recommend you to someone else?
...Call back?
...Invite you to return?
...Read your brochure?
...Call a customer for a reference?
...Give you a renewal date for their policy?
...Tell you how they make program decisions?
...Tell you who the decision-maker is?
...Disclose the brand of the product they now use?

You must know your objective or you may fall victim to the old saying, "Be careful what you ask for because you might get it."

> *I once successfully sent the message "try two techniques tomorrow" to a highly resistant journalist who was attending a workshop. I knew I was successful, because I called him the next day and asked him what he thought of the program. He responded, "I am skeptical, but I think I will try two techniques tomorrow and see what happens." Success!!*
>
> *Or was it?*
>
> *I had worded the command wrong. As a result, no change will ever take place. Why not? Tomorrow, this man will have the same message in his head, "Try two techniques tomorrow." Since tomorrow will always be a day away, eventually the command will be forgotten. You must say what you really want.*

Be sure your action command is achievable. It makes no sense to deliver a command to "buy" if the person is not authorized to buy. Instead, a command to "recommend" or "set up a meeting" with the decision-maker is more appropriate. Perhaps, the only achievable command may be "Talk about your current policy", "Tell me what your company really needs" or even "Describe how the decision will be made."

During the course of a sales call or presentation, you may change your objective several times. For instance, you may start out assuming your prospect can make a decision. As you gain rapport, you discover that your "new best friend" is not authorized to make a decision to buy. You must then change your objective and your action commands. What started out as an objective to "buy", for instance, now becomes an objective to "recommend". Your action commands must then change. Know what your audience *can* do and decide what you want done. Then say it.

NOTE:

Do not get greedy. You can only send a limited number of commands before a person will get confused and ignore you. Choose what you want and say it. This requires your knowing your outcome. You must know if you are asking someone to "buy", "decide", or "recommend". Choose an outcome that is possible. Even the best of words cannot create the impossible. If your prospect cannot sign the contract, there is no sense in trying to use a command to "sign" or "buy". Instead, go for what is possible.

USE ACTION WORDS

To create mental activity, you must choose words and phrases that are action phrases. Use what our high school English teachers called the "active voice." *"Looking forward to hearing from you"*, and *"You are getting the best with us"* are NOT action phrases. "Looking" and "Getting" are not verbs. They are not commands. Words ending in -ing do not create mental activity. You must use action words to create results.

Indirect commands do not create action. The memo that says "The smoking ban is now in effect" will not be as successful as one that says "Stop smoking." (The same memo will be even more effective if it says "You can smoke at home, but be a non-smoker on these premises") There are many stories of people being fired in such an indirect manner that they arrived for work the next day! If the action is not clear, the message will be lost.

In choosing an action command, it helps to visualize your audience. Then mentally point your finger at that person and tell him or her exactly what you want mentally done—*call me, talk to me, invite me to your office, decide to buy The Unfair Advantage*, or whatever else your objective may be. In this way, you can focus and identify what you want to say and what you want the person to do.

NOTE:

Use short words whenever possible. Do not make the mind work, or you invite resistance or inattention.

Say or write "*Do*"; avoid "*undertake*", "*participate*", or "*implement.*"

Say or write "*See*"; avoid "*observe*", "*perceive*", or "*visualize.*"

The only exception might be when repeating a command. If you have said it once in a short version, you can use longer words the second time to help mask your repetition.

PASS THE MANNEQUIN TEST

Another way to ensure a good action command is the "Mannequin Test." The "Mannequin Test" is simply the question: Can a mannequin do it? If your command can be successfully done by a mannequin, it is a poor command. It means the "command" is really not an action but a request to be passive. Passive commands will not create mental activity. A request to do nothing or to *stop* doing something is really a request to create a vacuum. Human beings cannot oblige.

Commands that fail the mannequin test frequently account for instructions or memos that get ignored. Too often, we ask people to *not* do something, and this is contrary to how people behave. Provide an alternative action rather than a request for inaction. Clarify the behavior or decision you want to occur.

For instance, *"Quit thinking about your problems"* is not likely to create mental activity. Only a mannequin can *not do* something. A mannequin can comply with the following commands:

> *"Don't hit your sister."*
> *"Quit worrying about tomorrow."*
> *"Be quiet."*

Instead, ask yourself "What do I want the person to *do*?" I want you to...

> ..."*Think about ways to solve this problem.*"
> ..."*Be nice to your sister.*"
> ..."*Concentrate on what went right today.*"
> ..."*Stop talking and read your book instead.*"

No mannequin can handle those commands.

131

SATISFY THE CONTEXT TEST

An action command is intended to create mental activity. Ideally, you want to create a message that survives after you have left. Therefore, the message must make sense on its own, independent of any specific context. It must stand alone. For instance, *"Remember us..."* will have no meaning once you are gone. Who is *"us"*? In the example earlier, if the manufacturing company's CEO had said *"Trust us"* instead of *"Trust ABCo."*, it is unlikely the customer would have called back with the words *"We feel we can trust ABCo."*

Instead of *"Remember us"*, a more effective phrase might be *"Remember the ABC company as you..."* Instead of saying *"Let's talk about how we might be able to help you in the future,"* change the words like this: *"Think about how Aztec Widgets can help in the future."* *"...Aztec Widgets can help..."* is the action command, and it makes sense on its own without your needing to be present to give it meaning.

SUMMARY

Action commands lead people to do what you want them to do. They are used to help people "mentally rehearse" the close or the decision you are seeking. With enough mental rehearsal, the final act will seem to come from them rather than from any active "closing" on your part. The best action commands are:

Short
Limited to one or two key ideas
Action oriented
Repeated in different ways

Once you know how to send an action command, the next challenge is to send it in a way that avoids resistance. Obviously, telling someone to *"Buy the ABC product"* will not usually make that person rush immediately to sign the contract. Most selling behavior includes a pattern of resistance and negotiation. When someone recognizes that a selling situation is taking place, conscious resistance is introduced. However, if you can send your message in a way that is not noticed, it can create mental activity without inviting the pattern of behavior and verbal responses usually associated with resistance. Without resistance, the likelihood of the desired behavior occurring is significantly increased. The process of sending a message without it being noticed is often called "subliminal." In NLP terms, it is called "embedding" the command which is the topic of the next chapter.

EXERCISE

Action Commands

Make the following statements into an action command:

1. "I am looking forward to hearing from you."

2. "The brochure is for you."

3. "We can be reached at 555-3241."

4. "We hope that attendance will no longer be a problem here."

5. "As always, it was a pleasure to talk with you again."

6. "Thanks for your inquiry. Enclosed is your packet..."

7. "Let us know what you think of the proposal."

8. "We know you have a choice in travel, and we thank you for choosing United."

Action Command Exercise: *Sample Answers*

1. "I am looking forward to hearing from you."
   *I **look forward to our talking**.*

2. "The brochure is for you."
   *As you **read the brochure**,...*

3. "We can be reached at 555-3241."
   ***Call Rogers Corp.** at 555-3421 when you need...*

4. "We hope that attendance will no longer be a problem here."
   ***Arrive on time** every day, and...*

5. "As always, it was a pleasure to talk with you again."
   *I **enjoy our talking together** and look forward to doing it again...*

6. "Thanks for your inquiry. Enclosed is your packet..."
   *Thank you for deciding to **call Ajax**. As you **look at the brochure**, ...*

7. "Let us know what you think of the proposal."
   *After you **read the proposal**, we will talk about the next step...*

8. "We know you have a choice in travel, and we thank you for choosing United."
   *We know you have options when you travel and we are glad you decided to **choose United**.*

EXERCISE

Mannequin Test

Replace these messages with phrases that will pass the "Mannequin Test" for action commands:

1. "Quit worrying about how hard this will be."

2. "Stop wasting your money."

3. "Be quiet."

4. "Avoid snap decisions."

5. "Wait until we can get together before making your mind up."

"Mannequin Test" Exercise: *Sample Answers*

1. "Quit worrying about how hard this will be."
   Begin to list your first steps toward a solution.

2. "Stop wasting your money."
   Save your money by...

3. "Be quiet."
   Concentrate on...

4. "Avoid snap decisions."
   Make your decision but gather the facts first...

5. "Wait until we can get together before making your mind up."
   Until we meet, think about this...

EXERCISE

Context Test

Rewrite these comments to satisfy the "Context Test":

1. "Keep us in mind if you ever need extruded widgets."

2. "You're not buying copiers, you are buying our service. We make the difference here."

3. "When you need insurance, give us a call."

4. "Recommend us. We can do the job."

"Context Test" Exercise: *Sample Answers*

1. "Keep us in mind if you ever need extruded widgets."
   When you need widgets, you remember Acme.

2. "You're not buying copiers, you are buying our service. We make the difference here."
   You're not going to decide to buy Ranier Copiers. You going to buy Susan Snyder—Susan Snyder is the difference between Ranier Copiers and the other brands.

3. "When you need insurance, give us a call."
   I know you do not want insurance. No one wants it, but when you need insurance, you will want EveryState.

4. "Recommend us. We can do the job."
   We appreciate your support for us. Keep that feeling, and talk up the Daley Group when Mr. Jones asks whom you recommend. Think about why you want the Daley Group and tell him.

11 Embedding the Action Command

"It is more fun to talk with someone who doesn't use long, difficult words but rather short, easy words like "What about lunch?" —from <u>Pooh's Little Instruction Book.</u>

INTRODUCTION

The best round of golf I played in my early golfing days began, as is often true, with a terrible drive. As my partner, a new client and president of a large mail-order business near Chicago, joined me for my second shot, he said, "This reminds me of a story.

"A struggling golfer, about your age and skill level, was having such a bad day he decided to kill himself. He threw down his clubs and began walking toward the lake next to the fairway. The caddie called after him, 'What are you doing?'

"'I'm going to drown myself in this lake and end my suffering forever.'

"'That won't work,' said the caddie. 'You can't drown in that lake. You don't keep your head down long enough.'"

140

"Keep your head down." That is what he told me to do, and that is what I did for the rest of the game. In NLP terms, *"Keep your head down"* is an action command. Yet, in most situations, if someone had directly said, "Duane, you need to keep your head down. You would play a lot better", I might have resisted or at least protested. I might have thought of reasons that "keep your head down" did not work for me or seemed too simplistic, or maybe I would have just cried out, "BUT I DO!!" Yet his subtle and indirect way of sending an action command bypassed the usual denial and resistance. (And my game improved!)

Even the best action commands will not automatically lead to the desired action. Sometimes people consciously resist. Other times, the message gets garbled and distorted as your audience tries to interpret or reword it to fit their bias or needs. To use words to lead or influence, you must engineer the message to avoid as much resistance and filtering as possible. You must learn to avoid being obvious—to hide the action command.

HIDE THE COMMAND

There is a tendency for people to hear what they want or expect to hear. They will also resist commands that are obvious. If someone tells you to "buy the APEX product", and you are a designated buyer for your company, you will resist. It is your job to resist. You will ignore the command and concentrate on improving your negotiation position. You will be wary and resistant.

Unless you do not notice the action command!

If a message can be sent that creates mental activity without conscious awareness, it can help lead someone toward the desired outcome without stirring up resistance.

"Unnoticed" commands are sometimes called "subliminal" commands. Unfortunately, the term "subliminal" has acquired negative connotations over the years. Unfounded claims of subliminal commands in advertising pictures, motion picture trailers, and self-help tapes have created a suspicion about anything that is labeled subliminal.

Recent research has even tried to debunk the notion of subliminal learning by demonstrating that subliminal influence only seems to last about 1/10th of a second in a laboratory test. Of course what is interesting to note, is that the research test revealed nearly 100% success in influencing subliminally the person's behavior under the right short-term conditions. Could it be the real interpretation of the research is *not* the failure of subliminal messages as a concept but the challenge to find ways to lengthen the obvious power of the process?

In other words, the research confirmed it works. Now, how do we make it last long enough to be useful?

Call the same process by another name—Unconscious Learning—and psychological research literature confirms that it exists. A recent summary of psychological research on the unconscious mind published by the American Psychological Association observed, "It is not a question of *whether* the unconscious mind can learn, but *how much* can it be taught?"

The key to unconscious learning, subliminal messages or unnoticed action commands is to hide or embed the message. Embedding a message means to mask the message so that it does not get noticed. It is a way of creating mental activity without generating resistance. The President of the manufacturing firm who delivered the embedded message "Trust ABCo" has a $5 million contract that says embedded messages work. My golf game attests to the fact that embedded messages work. To embed an action command, use one of the following techniques:

- **Embed in a negative**
- **Embed by redirecting attention**
- **Use natural inattention**
- **Embed by breaking the phrase**
- **Embed in a joke or story**

EMBED IN A NEGATIVE

The easiest way to hide or embed an action command is to use negatives. The mind must first process a positive action statement. Therefore, even if negatives are used, they do not prevent the mental activity. They only distract the conscious thinking process and help reduce resistance.

> *"Don't **decide to buy** from ABC yet. There are still questions to ask..."*
> *"Don't **say yes** yet. You haven't heard..."*
> *"You **should** not **decide to buy** before..."*

The use of a negative puts your audience at ease. They will not feel like you are pushing them. While a straight action command— *"Say yes"*—would be viewed as aggressive, *"Don't say yes yet"* will be received without the same feelings. Yet they both create the same mental activity.

Think about the message you really send when you say the following things to people:

> *Don't worry about being laid off."* (Worry!)
> *"Before you think about cost, I want to show you some features and benefits."* (And while you do, what are they thinking about...cost, just like you told them to do.)
> *"You'll never regret this purchase."* (How to invite buyer's remorse!)

"Don't forget to call Aunt Rose." (What was I supposed to do?)

Negatives fool the conscious mind. They enable you to send a message that does not get judged. It can even work on modifying your own behavior.

> *A client recently told me his secret to playing a good game of golf. He says to himself each time he is ready to drive, "Don't hit on the fairway." It takes the conscious pressure off and also directs the mind to program the muscles.*

EMBED WITH REDIRECTION

Magicians prevent us from seeing how a trick is done by directing our attention to where they want us to look. They attract our conscious mind while doing something else out of our awareness. "Word magicians" do the same thing. By directing the listener's or reader's attention toward something else, an action command can be delivered and not consciously noticed.

In the movie, *Roger Rabbit*, the evil villain was able to find Roger by knocking on the wall the rhythm to the familiar phrase "Shave and a haircut, two bits". By tapping only the "Shave and a haircut...", Roger could not resist the urge to complete the phrase by tapping out the final beats. It nearly killed him to not follow the lead of the rhythm pattern.

Just as the movie suggested, people cannot resist following a lead or completing a known pattern. The conscious mind follows an obvious lead. If I say, *"There are three important points here. One...",* it is nearly impossible not to attend and wait for the blank to be filled in.

A Chicago-based convenience store, White Hen Pantry, ran a brilliant radio commercial for several years. It used the sung phrase, "*When you run out, run out to White Hen.*" This phrase is sung several times during the ad. At the very end of the spot, the singer sings "*When you run out, run out to...*" and stops! It is irresistible and nearly impossible to not complete the phrase "*...run out to White Hen*", an embedded command that only exists in your mind as you sing it to yourself!

Attention can be redirected by using certain words that invite the conscious mind to follow. These words or phrases include:

* How to...
* If...
* Before...
* When...
* While...
* Although...
* Three things...(any number)
* ...Can you list one or two? (Or use any question linked to something other than the embedded command.)

Any student of traditional sales training programs will recognize that some of these words, especially "if" and "hope" are often criticized in a sales presentation. They are said to dilute the presentation and to create doubt in the mind of the buyer that you are really committed to your product or service. Unfortunately, such an accusation clearly misses the power of redirecting attention away from the embedded message.

> "*If you **sign the ABC contract**, there are several other issues we might want to consider. Can you think of one or two?*"
>
> "*How to **decide to buy the Krell Model X** is not an easy decision, and I'll tell you why...*"

> *"Before you recommend Alpha Corp. to your boss, let's look carefully at..."*
>
> *"While I hope you may feel good about Aztec Widget and want to buy right now, I suggest that there are still several questions that may..."*
>
> *"You can sign the contract or you can ask yourself, what else do I need to know? Can you think of more questions?"*

Words that misdirect attention take the edge off the command. They enable you to be forceful with words without being interpersonally forceful. Consequently, they avoid creating resistance.

NOTE:

When redirecting attention, it is important to say the whole thought smoothly. Avoid pausing. Especially avoid pausing after the action command. Your tone of voice must indicate that the really important things you are saying are about to be said. Let your voice indicate the anticipation as you move forward, away from the embedded action command.

NOT: "You can sign the contract...(pause) or you can ask yourself, what else do I need to know? (Pause) What questions do you have?"

INSTEAD: "You can sign the contract or you can ask yourself, what else do I need to know? What questions do you have?" (Pause now.)

USE NATURAL INATTENTION

The average person's attention span is short. That is why no one listens very well to what someone else is saying to you. And the more someone talks, the easier it is to "tune them out." As a result, you can embed a command by simply hiding it in a lot of words. The famous hypnotist/therapist Milton Erickson, who served as a model for many of the NLP methods, could put people in a hypnotic trance by flooding them with words. His patients would not be aware of what he was telling them to do. They would comply, however.

We have accomplished similar results in telemarketing. One experimental script began with three long run-on phrases. Embedded in the phrases was the command "talk to me" several times. The phrase would then end with the "invitation" phase of the selling process: "Is this a good time to talk to me, or would you prefer to talk to me at another time?" More than 50% of those called granted permission to continue. In most cases, it is estimated that very few even realized what they were being asked, having been put in a semi-trance with the wordiness of the script while being told to "talk".

Embedding in a flood of words is most effective in a verbal form. It works less well in writing, because people will not read the text.

• End of a Letter

There are other times when people do not pay attention and action commands can be inserted with little risk of being noticed. The easiest of these is the end of a letter. How many people actually reflect on the phrase "*I am looking forward to hearing from you*" or "*Thanks for your interest*"? The line that precedes "Sincerely" is rarely read consciously. Therefore, it is

NOTE:

The trick to embedding with many words is to be somewhat theatrical in your delivery. Use your voice to sound interesting and enthusiastic. Let your pitch rise and fall, even if your words are not really that interesting. Vary the speed of your delivery. When you get to an embedded command, drop your tone just enough to emphasize the command but not enough to be noticed! Then go immediately back to your original tone and pace. You are using your voice, not necessarily your words, to invite your audience to follow you and, therefore, not notice your embedded command.

Also, avoid pausing in predictable places, such as at the end of a sentence or phrase. Such pauses can trigger your audience to react before you really want them to. Interrupt the normal pattern by pausing in unusual places. This will actually help keep your commands unnoticed. Try practicing on the following script:

"We hope you have seen enough today to feel you can use one technique and hear yourself interacting with others in a more effective way. But we don't want you to use one technique for the wrong reasons. You want to persuade while being ethical too. After you use one technique and discover how powerful you can be when you choose to be, you will enjoy your choices and find new places to use one more technique, maybe on a new audience."

an excellent opportunity to send an action command—one that is embedded in inattention. It is important, as with all action commands, that the words are truly commands. *"I am looking forward to hearing from you"* is NOT a command. Instead, close with *"I look forward to our talking"*. Instead of *"Thanks for your interest"*, use a command such as *"I am pleased to know you have interest in Amalgamated Ratchets."*

• On-hold Messages

Another opportunity to use inattention to deliver an unnoticed action command is the on-hold message on telephones. Very few companies have discovered the opportunity of sending action commands to their captive audience that is not paying any attention to the sounds coming from the phone. The conscious mind is focused on hearing the voice they seek or rehearsing what the person is going to say when the voice finally comes on the phone. What a perfect time to send a message!

Instead of "Ask our service representative about our new and improved Cosmic Juicer", decide what you want a caller to do or believe and say it. For instance, *"If you **want** to see the **Cosmic Juicer** in your stores, ask the manager. Call the owner. **Ask for Cosmic Juicer.** We are sorry you are on hold and you know this is not what we **want. Cosmic Juicer** is eager to hear from our customers and we hope you will not have to wait long.*

Watch for other opportunities to utilize inattention. For example, when a United Airlines plane lands, we hear, "We know you have a choice in air travel, and we thank you for choosing United." Why not *"We know you have choices, and we are glad you decided to **choose United.**"*?

EMBED BY BREAKING THE PHRASE

Still another way to embed a command is to break the phrase into parts. Notice the example above, especially "...this is not what we want. Cosmic Juicer..." This is an example of a command message broken apart. The ear does not hear the familiar verb-noun pattern, yet the brain can notice it. A slight verbal pause at the command helps make it work, but the breaking of the pattern can also be effective in written communication. *"...to help you **decide. To buy American Widgets** is one way to..." "On any given day, there are many things you must **decide. To buy Karma Soap** probably is not the biggest decision of the day; I'm sure you can think of bigger ones...yet..."*

EMBED IN A STORY OR JOKE

One of the most effective and powerful ways to embed a message is to use a joke or story. If you are a natural story-teller, then this skill can be a powerful tool for you. If you are not adept at story-telling, you may want to choose not to use this technique.

The power of a joke or story is its psychological similarity to the actual command. Recall the golf story told earlier. It contained the embedded command *"Keep your head down."* It also set the stage by linking the story to me with "parallel parts" or pieces of the story that resemble either the immediate situation or people. In the golf story, the story was not about *me*. Instead, it was about someone who was *"about your age and skill level."* The golfer in the story was also frustrated, linking his/her feeling state to mine at that specific time. By linking the parts of the story to the issues or people at hand, a story or joke can be a powerful tool of persuasion.

When I conduct a team-building project with executive teams, I often begin with a long story that begins with people trying to outwit and embarrass others. The story ends with the statement, "The solution is in your hands." Most participants assume my story is an awkward attempt to tell a joke, even though the story is not funny. The audience usually advises me to avoid joke-telling in the future.

Inevitably, by the end of the day, when the team members are engaged in some heated problem-solving and begin to blame each other for their problems, at least one person will volunteer "We aren't going to get anywhere blaming someone else. **The solution is in our hands.** *"*

One secret to successful story-telling is to avoid interpretation. The power of a metaphor is in the vacuum it creates. If a story is interpreted, it loses its power and becomes subject to resistance and filtering. Religions have always known the power of a good story, yet ministers constantly find it necessary to analyze and interpret in detail the greatest stories of them all. There is a great scene in the movie *Cinema Paradisio* where the old man is advising the young boy on love. He tells a long story that has no moral, and when he finishes it, he stands and announces, *"I don't know what it means. And if you figure it out, you tell me."* It is the mental struggle to understand that accounts for the power of the metaphor. By the time someone can grasp the meaning, the mental rehearsal has bypassed resistance.

Sometimes metaphors can make a message more acceptable to an audience.

I once worked with an accounting department that was isolated from the rest of the company. Their input was ignored and their impact on the business was far below what it should have been. They had difficulty getting flash reports, forecast updates, or even budget figures, and attempts to control inventories or costs were fruitless. On examination, I discovered that the company culture embraced a military metaphor. Projects were launched, problems were attacked, teams brought weapons to bear on problems, schedules and competitors were the enemy, and so on. Yet, none of the members of the accounting group had any military background or embraced the language. We spent a half-day translating their desired messages into the culturally dictated metaphor. Now they could ask for scouting reports, debriefings, a lay-of-the-land while also reminding managers not to out-run their supplies or charge ahead without considering the cost of the campaign. Their effectiveness increased ten-fold.

Embedding messages through stories, jokes, or metaphors is difficult. It requires much practice. The concept is important, nevertheless, not only because of its potential power, but also because if you are a joke teller, you must guard against inadvertently sending wrong messages. The story is a powerful source of influence. Be careful.

EXERCISE

Embedded Commands #1

Hide the following commands in sentences using negatives:

1. Buy Aztec Widgets

2. Recommend this proposal

3. Trust me

4. Look for continuous improvement

Embedded Commands Exercise: *Sample Answers*

1. Buy Aztec Widgets
>   *"I don't want you to buy Aztec Widgets without considering the sound benefits that you can see here..."*
>   *"Don't buy Aztec Widgets just because I say so..."*

2. Recommend this proposal
>   *"You are not going to recommend this proposal without having plenty of documentation to support your recommendation..."*
>   *"You can't recommend this proposal just on what you see here..."*

3. Trust me
>   *"People like you don't trust me the minute I put on a badge that says 'consultant'. I know that. I don't expect you to trust me until..."*

4. Look for continuous improvement
>   *"You can't look for continuous improvement until you know what to look for. People don't just get up one morning and say , "I'm going to look for continuous improvement opportunities today.""*

EXERCISE

Embedded Commands #2

Hide the following commands in sentences using words or phrases hidden by redirecting attention:

1. Buy Aztec Widgets

2. Recommend this proposal

3. Trust me

4. Look for continuous improvement

Embedded Commands #2 Exercise:
Sample Answers

1. Buy Aztec Widgets

   *"How to **buy Aztec Widgets** can be an easy process if at least two steps are assured..."* (Why would you want to avoid saying, "Buying Aztec Widgets does not have to be difficult..."?)

2. Recommend this proposal

   *"There are at least three issues to consider before you might **want to recommend** this proposal..."* (Help the person follow the anticipated pattern and focus on "three issues" by emphasizing *"First..."* and then, perhaps, pausing before continuing.)

3. Trust me

   *"Before you can **trust Duane Lakin** or anyone else, that trust must be earned, and there are several ways..."*

4. Look for continuous improvement

   *"I want to show you several ways to **look for continuous improvement,** and they are, One..."*

EXERCISE

Embedded Commands #3

Rephrase the following ideas to send an embedded action command. Use any of the techniques for embedding that you wish. (Use VAK enrichment when possible.) Remember to ask: "What do I want the reader/listener to *do*?"

1. "Thanks for the request. Enclosed is your packet..."

2. "As you can see, this is a great proposal. Let us know what you think."

3. "We make it our business to know your business. We meet your needs. We have the capabilities to make you competitive by combining our resources."

Embedded Commands #3 Exercise:
Sample Answers

1. "Thanks for the request. Enclosed is your packet..."

> *I am pleased to hear you **have interest** in Acme. If you **look at the enclosed brochure**, be sure to turn to page 9 and notice the three things we talked about yesterday...*

2. "As you can see, this is a great proposal. Let us know what you think."

> *I now have a better feel for what you **want**. **Copious Notes** has experience in this area, and I hope we can help you get what **you need**. **Copious Notes** prides itself on service as our customers can easily tell you. Give me a call when you **want** us at **Copious Notes** to answer more of your questions. I **look forward to our talking**.*

3. "We make it our business to know your business. We meet your needs. We have the capabilities to make you competitive by combining our resources."

> *Before you **call Beta Brokers**, we **want to talk** about your business, not ours. We do not want a **call** to **Beta Brokers** to be a sales call. Instead, we want it to be like one partner has a question for another partner and makes a **call**. **Beta Brokers** is a large family of brokers with offices in...*

12 *Mindsets (Metaprograms)*

"There is no truth. There is only perception." —Gustave Flaubert

INTRODUCTION

You are a consultative seller, and you are trying to propose a solution to a problem. You have met with five key people and offered your ideas. Unfortunately, each person gave you a different response. The following is what each said:

> *"I don't know. I'm concerned about the problems in that division already."*
>
> *"What other choices are there? Is this the only way you think will work?"*
>
> *"Who else has done this? What was their experience like?"*
>
> *"How do you propose we actually start and what is the specific plan?"*
>
> *"Hmm. I think we should try something different. Suppose we…"*

Each of these comments is a hint about how the person thinks. It reflects the bias or preconceptions of the person in your audience and not the content of your idea. To sell each of these people, you would need to adapt or "engineer" your message in a slightly different way for each presentation. But in what way? How should you change what you say to match each person's view of his/her world?

The answer can be found in your understanding of MIND-SETS—the maps a person uses to think about his/her environment. MINDSETS (or Metaprograms as they are called in NLP literature) can be complex, and you will be more successful selling your ideas when you understand how to match your words to multiple MINDSETS. When you discover someone's thinking process is driven by one or more MINDSET, you will have a great advantage as a seller.

NOTE:

One comment by itself is not sufficient to draw a conclusion. But if you listen carefully, the comments each person makes can shed light on how to prepare your next presentation to that person to get his/her approval for your proposal.

THE BRAIN AND MINDSETS

Your brain wants to be efficient. It looks for ways to draw conclusions fast and respond to new information quickly. In doing so, it learns shortcuts. This can be good or bad, depending on the situation. In most cases, it leads us to have biases or preconceived ideas about how things are or should be. By

160

seeking efficiency, however, we often lose the ability to notice and listen effectively. We "jump to conclusions" or overly generalize information in order to make our decision. Efficient? Yes. Effective? Not always.

Your brain tends to seek efficiency at the cost of accuracy. You learn to delete information that seems unimportant at the time. You hear what you want to hear. You learn to choose what to look at and what to ignore. If new information does not fit what you expect, you may distort it and force it to fit your expectations. You often simply block out or reinterpret what you do not expect to find or do not want to have to integrate into your existing beliefs. You tend to be open to ideas that fit what you already believe and resistant to things you hear that are contrary to your biases. This is normal and necessary to be able to live in a world in which you are constantly bombarded with new information. You develop a shortcut for handling too much information. You usually are not aware of how your shortcut works, however. It is not part of your conscious thinking process, yet it greatly impacts your decisions.

Your brain is often lazy. When you hear a word or statement that is vague, a vacuum is created. Rather than seeking to understand, you are apt to generalize and fill the vacuum with your beliefs and assumptions. This is just human nature. The human brain cannot tolerate a vacuum of information, whether it is accurate or not. As a result, a politician can announce the need for "change", and people will define "change" in ways that they believe it means without ever learning what the politician really means or believes. It is easier and quicker than asking or searching for an answer.

As result, over time you develop a "model" of the world around you. This model is based on what you have learned to expect rather than what you actually experience, because your expectations greatly filter your experience. As a result, it is not an accurate model. But it is close enough to be efficient. (In NLP terminology, this phenomenon is described with the phrase, "The map is not the territory.") A problem arises, however, when two or more people are trying to communicate, because everyone has a slightly different model from everyone else. Your model—or your combination of perceptions and biases and expectations and values and distortions and generalizations—are your Mindsets. Their combination is unique to you and different from the profiles of others.

In order for you to understand me, you need to understand my assumptions or Mindsets. Also, in order for you to see how to persuade or sell me, you need to know how to present your ideas in a format that matches my Mindsets. Failure to do so will lead to increased resistance to your ideas. Similar to the power of "VAK Matching", "Mindset Matching" enables you to reduce resistance and increase the likelihood of selling your proposal.

NOTE:

Mindsets tend to be context sensitive. You may display one set of behaviors at work, for instance, and different set at home.

Mindsets can be recognized by noticing what someone says and how someone behaves. By knowing what to ask and what to notice, you can identify many Mindsets patterns.

> ## NOTE:
>
> **VAK preferences are actually a type of Mindset. However, because of their importance to the overall application of NLP skills to sales, they have been given a separate focus in this book and in most NLP discussions.**

RECOGNIZING MINDSETS

Mindsets are often labeled in NLP terminology as opposites or contrasts on some linear measure:

TOWARD...........AWAY FROM
THINKER..........FEELER
OPTIMIST........PESSIMIST

This terminology is a little misleading, because it suggests that such extreme orientations are typical. This is not true. *For most metaprograms or Mindsets, the majority of people function in the middle of the metaprogram range.* Being in the middle range can, in fact, can be labeled as "BOTH", because it allows for flexibility and an openness to what is happening at that specific time and place. The context of a situation can influence which "end" of the continuum you may lean at a given time. As you gain more insight into yourself, you can learn to use the value of both parts of any Mindset continuum and "speak" whichever "language" fits best for the particular situation. Such flexibility is the goal of your gaining insight and awareness of your own Mindset profile. Adaptability to others is the goal of your gaining insight into others Mindsets.

When a Mindset is observed at either extreme of the continuum, that insight is valuable information for any seller. An extreme Mindset bias drives the behavior of the individual and heavily influences what a person sees and hears as well as how the person makes decisions. It is a powerful filter. An extreme Mindset is a signal for you that tells you to adjust the presentation of your ideas and proposals for that individual. You must respect the other person's filter and engineer your message to fit it.

Some authors have identified as many as 150 or more Mindsets. This simply means that careful observation of human behavior has led to noticing many patterns of behavior that can influence a person's functioning. However, from a practical perspective, such a large list is not helpful. You cannot be selling a product or service and also be expected to recognize 150 or even 20 patterns of behavior. Perhaps, over time, working with the same buyer or customer for many years, you can identify more subtle Mindsets, but for the purpose of this book, we will focus only on six Mindsets. They are called:

TOWARD/AWAY FROM
INTERNAL/EXTERNAL
OPTIONS/PROCEDURES
SAME/DIFFERENT
PROACTIVE/REACTIVE
GENERAL/SPECIFIC

The way to identify the six Mindsets is to listen and watch. Each Mindset has some helpful "Discovery Questions" to guide you. These are questions that can usually be asked in the course of a normal business discussion to help you determine if a driving Mindset—one that actively filters perception and influences behavior—is present. If you learn to include these

Discovery Questions into your interview, you will gather much useful information from your prospect or customer.

NOTE:

It is important to recognize that every Mindset has value in the right situation. It is always tempting to judge Mindsets, especially those that are different from your own patterns of acting or talking. Avoid this temptation! Every Mindset has value in the right situation. It is only when a Mindset begins to color everything you do that it becomes a liability rather than an asset. Do not judge; simply use your insights to be a better leader and seller. And as you discover your own Mindsets, ask yourself—How can I expand my awareness and overcome my own filters?

As you look at the Mindsets that follow, ask yourself, "Who do I know that is like this? What does he/she say or do that makes me think this? Have I matched his/her Mindset when I work with this person? If not, how could I do a better job of matching?"

Also, keep in mind that even if someone shows signs of several Mindsets, there is typically one or two that are the real power behind that person's decision-making. They are most influential in the person's behavior and attitudes. Try to determine which Mindsets are the real driving forces for the individual and focus your message engineering on those Mindsets as much as possible.

NOTE:

When you begin engineering your message to match Mindsets, include what you know about VAK language preferences, too. Combine VAK matching with Mindset matching whenever possible for the strongest and most persuasive communication.

And most important, as you work with the six Mindsets, look at each and ask yourself, "Where am I on this list? Do I have a regular bias or habit of working with problems that might fit one or more of the Mindsets? If so, how does that impact my work with others?" If you can learn more about yourself as well as others, your effectiveness will increase dramatically.

It is an assumption (Mindset?) in business that people are goal-oriented. This is probably true, but the word "goal" is as vague as "change." What does your customer want to accomplish? Is he/she trying to achieve something or avoid something? What goal is desired by your client or prospect that your product or service can help achieve? These are critical questions to ask if you are to be successful.

MINDSETS: TOWARD / AWAY FROM

The TOWARD customer is moving toward a specific outcome or achievement. He/she talks about a desire to reach a new objective or attain a new level of quality. Goals are clearly seen and priorities easily made, because the value of each goal is clear. Possibilities are embraced and pursued. The TOWARD person is the poster child for MBOs and objective-driven organizations. The TOWARD person responds well to incentives linked to specific outcomes.

A person with a TOWARDS orientation often focuses on goals and targets, especially "stretch" goals. At times, goals can take the place of real plans and lead to an unrealistic charge up a dangerous hill. Still, much progress in business is done by those with a TOWARDS orientation. The TOWARDS leader with at least a five-year scope of thinking is apt to be a strong CEO for a healthy organization that wants to grow. Sales managers are often TOWARDS leaders as they set quotas and push people for results.

An AWAY FROM person has a completely different definition of "goal." He/she is looking to avoid a problem or get rid of an unpleasant situation. An AWAY FROM person is quick to see problems and anticipate barriers. He/she looks for problems if they are not immediately obvious and may only feel comfortable when a problem is found. Deadlines can motivate an AWAY FROM person, because he/she does not want the problem of being late. Such a person is often motivated by the fear of losing a job or being controlled by outside forces. He/she is motivated by knowing that such problems are being prevented.

Someone with an AWAY FROM tendency will focus on finding, avoiding, or preventing problems. They are often astute at considering potential pitfalls in a plan. They are also quick to see when something is not working well. They are alert to what could happen and act to prevent such a problem. They will be quicker to talk about a problem than to recognize someone for an accomplishment. They are more likely to be motivated by charting errors or costs and seeing reductions than by charting growth.

Based on Roger Bailey's research in what he calls the "Language and Behavior Profile", approximately 40% of the population is TOWARDS, 40% of the population is AWAY FROM, and 20% are in the middle. Keep in mind, however, that his population was largely North American based, and cultures can differ in their preferences for Mindsets.

For several years, I worked with a client who was very conservative and reluctant to try new things. Yet he constantly spoke about his desire to achieve certain revenue goals and how he wanted to grow his business. On one occasion, I presented him with seven proposed goals for the coming year, including "Identify successors to key leaders" and "Create a new selection standard to improve the quality of sales people." He showed little interest in such goals and cited concerns with cost and approach.

As I analyzed why he would resist such suggestions, I finally realized the extent of his "AWAY FROM" Mindset. He was an individual who felt good when he could find a problem. He rarely praised good performance but was quick to counsel poor performance. He was amazingly tolerant of people who made mistakes but corrected them. No one would get fired for a really bad outcome if the problem was fixed. At the same time, no one really got recognized for outstanding performance or creativity. There was always another problem that needed attention. Problems brought out the best in him, and the prevention of problems was his driving motivation.

With this insight, I again met with him to propose the EXACT SAME seven goals but with a different approach. For instance, instead of "Iden-

tify successors", I suggested a plan to prepare for the "Mack Truck scenario" in which key people might get hit by a truck. I emphasized the need to avoid a vacancy that would exist and could impact the business in a negative fashion. Instead of "Create a new selection standard to improve quality", I suggested a "New selection model to reduce the number of sales people who failed to thrive." He was enthusiastic about all the new proposals and agreed to the plan.

WORDS TO NOTICE

A person who is biased in a TOWARDS direction is likely to say things such as the following:

> "We can achieve this."
> "I want to double our sales this decade."
> "I am not afraid to risk a little to win a lot."
> "I want to increase sales."
> "Our business will always be profitable."
> "Our sales are up 20%"

A person who is biased in an AWAY FROM direction is likely to say things such as the following:

> "I want to avoid a crisis."
> "No bank can control my business, because I will never owe a lot of money."
> "We must be vigilant and watch for problems that can impact us."
> "Our costs are down 20% and I need to keep them down."

NOTE:

Traditionally, sales managers look for sales candidates who are "goal oriented" or "achievement driven." They offer goals, quotas, and incentives to drive selling behavior. However, much research suggests that the very best sellers are driven by fear! They fear that their last sale was, indeed, their very last one and next week will not be as productive. Fear of having no sales drives them to work harder. If that is the case, sales managers would be wise to seek AWAY FROM candidates rather than those goal-driven TOWARD candidates that are typically sought.

DISCOVERY QUESTIONS

Typical Discovery Questions would be:

- What do you want to happen? Why is that important?
- How will you know if you have been successful?
- What will this have accomplished for you?
- Why is that accomplishment important for you?
- What are you trying to accomplish or prevent?
- In six months, how will you know if you have made the right decision?

SELLING HINTS

As you already know, the key to getting the unfair advantage is Message Engineering™—engineering your message to fit your audience. In this case, you need to find a way to say your ideas or proposal in either "AWAY FROM" language or "TOWARDS" language if you have a specific individual as your audience. As with VAK, if you do not know the preference of your audience, you will have a stronger advantage if you engineer your words for both Mindsets.

With a TOWARDS audience, you need to use words like "goals", "achieve", and "opportunity." You may want to use phrases such as the following:

> "In six months, you will see an increase in your sales."
> "This will help you achieve that $100 million goal you announced two years ago."
> "As you have heard, we can help you outpace your competition in both regions."
> "By combining this policy with an investment tool, you will be able to see an increase in your retirement fund while also owning insurance."
> "You customers will be much happier with this new model because of the energy savings as well as the quality of the output."

With an AWAY FROM audience, you will want to says things like "prevent", "solve", or "avoid." You may want to use phrases such as the following:

> "This will help you prevent such losses in the future."

"This house will keep your son from having to walk so far to a good school."

"Our approach will avoid having to return to court in six months to renegotiate."

"By having this policy, your family's future will be protected against disaster if something were to happen to you."

"You will have far fewer customer complaints once this is installed."

To reach an unknown or larger audience and to ensure that both extremes are matched, you want to combine the two "languages" by saying things such as the following:

"This policy can help in two ways: First, it provides income protection for your family in case you were to be ill for an extended period of time and unable to earn income. Second, it also has a return-of-premium feature that can act as a savings plan for you in the event you stay healthy. It is like a savings program to add to your retirement fund."

"Our new machine will reduce your service costs by at least 15%. In addition, the energy savings alone will help you attract new customers."

EXERCISE

Toward / Away From

1. Describe the benefits of one of your products or services for an AWAY FROM person.

2. Describe the benefits of one of your products or services for a TOWARD person.

Label the following statements or behaviors as TOWARDS or AWAY FROM:

1. "I want a vacation to get away from it all."

2. "I want a home that will give me a place to escape from the hassles of the day."

3. "I want a home close to good schools."

4. "I want to quit smoking."

5. "I want to be a non-smoker."

6. "I want to lose weight."

7. "I want to be better toned and have less than 10% body fat."

ANSWERS

1. AF   3. T   5. T   7. T

2. AF   4. AF   6. AF

MINDSETS: INTERNAL/EXTERNAL

Everyone reacts differently when asked to evaluate a situation or even another person. Where does the standard or measurement for evaluation come from? Where does the "frame-of-reference" for making that judgment originate?

Typically, the frame comes from either within yourself or from outside yourself. You either use internal standards or some outside "authority" to make the judgment.

For someone with an INTERNAL Mindset, the frame of reference comes from within. INTERNALS tend to make their own decisions before they check to see what others think. They "just know" what needs to be done or what is best. They may ask for information, but in the end, the final decision belongs to them. An INTERNAL often uses the word "I" in conversations.

INTERNAL people are often independent and decisive in character. They tend to not like being told what to think or do. They dislike being closely managed, and they will resist attempts to tell them what they should decide. They do not like having a sales person telling them, "This is the right choice for you, sir." The INTERNAL will know the right choice, not the sales person.

An EXTERNAL is more likely to invite the opinions of others before making a decision. He/she will look for evidence of such opinions, such as a survey or recommendation. EXTERNALS will ask for guidance or advice. They must be careful, however, to avoid being too dependent on outside information. The EXTERNAL often uses the word "You" in conversations.

An EXTERNAL is apt to be interactive and more team oriented than some. They invite input and want to know what others are thinking. They are also more inclined to read reports and reviews of products and services. They can be influenced by the recommendations of others.

Based on Bailey's research with the LAB Profile, 40% of the population are INTERNALS, 40% are EXTERNALS, and 20% fall in the middle.

> *Compare the personal styles of Donald Trump and Bill Clinton. Do you think Trump, an INTERNAL, really cares what his colleagues say on his* Apprentice *show? He may look like he is listening, but he draws his own conclusions and makes up his own mind. He could care less if the press does not like his decisions about beauty queens or project managers. After all, he is THE DONALD.*
>
> *Mr. Clinton, an EXTERNAL, was often characterized as having to check the morning surveys before he could make a decision. Being popular was very important to him when he was in the White House, and there is little reason to believe the trend has changed today. He "feels our pain" and wants to do what the audience wants him to do. He tends to be a people-pleaser, and he runs a risk of being dependent on popular opinion to know what he wants to do. He judges situations based on what others say and feel.*

WORDS TO NOTICE

A person who is biased in an INTERNAL direction is likely to say things such as the following:

> "I just know."
> "It just feels right, and I trust my gut."
> "I have a good sense of what needs to be done. I just feel it."

"I don't really need to ask him. I already know what I want done."

"I appreciate your thoughts, but I have already made up my mind."

"Last time, my intuition was good. I am going to trust it again this time."

A person who is biased in an EXTERNAL direction is likely to say things such as the following:

"Let me look at the data first."

"What did they find at the other location?"

"Let me ask my team and see what they think."

"I won't vote until I see what the real data tells us."

"Do you have some research to support that claim?"

"How about references...can I talk to some of your customers?"

DISCOVERY QUESTIONS

Helpful Discovery Questions for INTERNAL/EXTERNAL Mindsets would be:

- "How do you typically make a decision like this?"
- The last time you changed your vendor for this product, how did you make that decision?"
- "What kind of information do you want to help you make this decision?"
- Is there someone you go to that helps you make decisions like this or do you tend to just know what to do?

SELLING HINTS

With an INTERNAL audience, it is important to avoid telling the prospect or client what he/she should think or do. Instead, use phrases such as the following:

- "Obviously, you will make this decision on your own. What do you want from me to help?"
- "What are you thinking? What questions are you still asking yourself?"
- "What would you recommend?"

With an EXTERNAL, use phrases such as the following:

- "What supporting data would you like to see?"
- "Would you like to talk with one of our customers?"
- "What have you heard from your colleagues about this?"
- "The field results have been excellent. Would you like to see them?"

For BOTH or in-between people and for an unknown audience, use phrases such as the following:

- "I would be glad to show you some references, but I'm guessing you have heard enough to make up your mind at this point."
- "It is obviously your decision, but I would be glad to provide some lab reports for you to study if that would help."

EXERCISE

Internal / External

1. Describe the benefits of one of your products or services for an INTERNAL person.

2. Describe the benefits of one of your products or services for a EXTERNAL person.

Label the following statements or behaviors as INTERNAL or EXTERNAL:

1. "I'm impressed."

2. "I need to ask the team."

3. "That's not going to be popular."

4. "I have a good feeling about this."

5. "This is not what I had in mind."

6. "Got any proof?"

ANSWERS

1. I
2. E
3. E
4. I
5. I
6. E

MINDSETS: OPTIONS/PROCEDURES

When you are confronted with a task to complete or a puzzle to solve, how do you think about it? How do you reason through the problem? Do you continually look for alternatives or do you hope to find a well-documented approach that works reliably? When you bought your last piece of electronic equipment, did you read the manual or just begin to explore?

WHY do you make the choices you make? Why did you take the job you have? Why did you follow a particular path on your last travel vacation? Why did you decide to buy your last car? Why did you pick choose your last realtor or attorney?

Your answers to these questions may help you discover whether you like options and choices or whether you prefer a familiar, tried-and-true approach. This set of opposite traits is the OPTIONS/PROCEDURES Mindset.

NOTE:

In the Enneagram profiling system, Type Seven is a classic OPTIONS person. A Seven wants to find creative options. He/she resists committing to one thing, because there are always other doors to open. The drive to find fun by being creative and free of having to do things the right way is a driving motivation for the Seven Type. It is more fun to start something new than to finish something that has become boring or routine, so projects often get started without being completed. Such characteristics are common with most OPTIONS people.

OPTIONS oriented people like to have choices. Even if they think they have found a good choice, they may keep looking at other possibilities. Even if they have a set of directions or a recipe to follow, they are unlikely to stick to the script. They like to improvise and try different things. On one day, they will do something one way; on the next day, a different way. The ability to be different is important to such people. They are not necessarily interested in hearing what has worked for others. They want choices.

NOTE:

It is a good idea to remember that an OPTIONS person is apt to find a PROCEDURES person dull and unduly compulsive. A PROCEDURES person often finds an OPTIONS person to be distractible, unclear, and too much like the negative stereotype of a smoke-and-mirrors salesperson.

A PROCEDURES customer will find it hard to trust an OPTIONS seller, because there will be too few details to support the claims for benefits. In addition, the typical OPTIONS seller will offer several different approaches in case the customer does not like the first one. PROCEDURES buyers will not react well to such a mismatched approach.

An OPTIONS person may develop a system to solve a problem, but if he/she sees or believes the problem has changed, the system will be abandoned in favor of a different or better idea. They often ask, "Why?", when told that something needs to be done a certain way. They tend to dislike routines and rules, and they often stretch the limits of the environment whenever possible. They are not afraid to break, or at least bend, the rules. They are the people who turn in expense reports late, "delegate up" whenever possible, and like to improvise as a style of working. They are often creative but sometimes hard to control. They are often energetic and motivated, especially at the beginning of a project or discussion while the possibility of options still exists.

PROCEDURES people, when faced with a decision, want to choose the "safe" approach. They like standards and rules to follow. They want to see what has worked in the past as a predictor for what will work in the future. They enjoy a set of steps to follow. They prefer scripts rather than being spontaneous. They want to know how things should be done and what is the right way. "That's beyond my pay grade" was probably first said by a PROCEDURES person.

A person with a PROCEDURES Mindset will often be methodical in behavior. Such a person is apt to expect to find a right way to do things and will ask, "What is right?" They often need you to be very clear about how to start the process, both the process of <u>buying</u> as well as the process of <u>implementing</u> your proposal.

If something gets started, they want to finish it. They often plan carefully Doing something correctly is almost as important as the outcome. They are sometimes more concerned with how something is done than why. They may find themselves lost or stuck until they can see the steps needed to get the job completely done. Most important, they want to know what has worked in the past and how they can ensure that doing it again in the exact same way will lead to the exact same results. When we choose general surgeons and airline pilots, we probably hope they are PROCEDURES people.

Based on Roger Bailey's LAB research, approximately 40% of the population are OPTIONS people, 40% are PROCEDURES people, and 20% are in the middle.

NOTE:

Andrew Bradbury (In <u>Develop Your NLP Skills</u>) points out, "A person in options mode really doesn't need motivating as self-motivation is one of their strengths; rather they need to be kept firmly (but not too obviously) on track. A person in procedures mode is best motivated if they are given detailed instructions, the need to make choices is minimized, and they can earn praise when they adhere to the standard procedures."

I know a company that screens via a test for self-motivated, hard-charging sales people. It then provides a highly procedure-based training including checklists for interviewing and a detailed set of procedures for making proposals with very limited decision discretion. Consistently, their best producers are disciplined people who do well with direction and rules to follow (or have found a sales manager that will allow them to delegate up). They often come from the Customer Service side of the business rather than from outside the company. The same people are their top performers year after year while the new hires come and go, because they fit the test but not the real job.

WORDS TO NOTICE

A person who is biased in an OPTIONS direction is likely to say things such as the following:

"I had several choices and I decided to take this one."

"I want to know my options and then I can make a well-informed choice."

"I like to find something a little different or challenging."

"I don't want to rush into a decision without hearing what is available."

"Can we tweak that plan a bit?"

"I supposed I could do ...."

"I can try this or that, right?"

A person with a PROCEDURES Mindset is likely to say things such as the following:

"When I first started on this, I began by..."

"How do you ever get that implemented?"

"I need a clear plan, a road map to follow."

"How successful has this been with others?

"Show me the whole plan, not just pieces. I need the whole picture."

"I can't see how to get started on this."

"This is how it should be done, right?"

"I must have a clear sense of how this actually can be done."

DISCOVERY QUESTIONS

Typical Discovery Questions would include the following:

- "Why did you decide to seek outside professionals for this project?"
- "Why did you choose to ask for proposals for this work?"
- "Do you think there is one best approach or are there many that might work?"
- "Are you looking for new methods or for an approach that is proven and tested?"
- "What does your typical day look like?"
- "How do you do your job?"

SELLING HINTS

To match the orientation of an OPTIONS person, it is important to respect his/her need for alternatives and control. You can be enthusiastic as you describe options, but do not try to oversell one over another. Let the customer make the choice. You are safe to describe the pros and cons of different approaches as long as you can stay fairly objective.

With an OPTIONS person, is it useful to say words such as, "opportunity", "new", and "not typical but we can do it for you."

"There are several choices for you to look at."

"Each of these options have its own set of advantages."

"Even though this is a standard model, I can
make several adjustments if you need them."

"That is one way we could proceed; fortunately, there are several others."

"We are very flexible as to how to modify
the standard model for you."

If your customer or prospect is a PROCEDURES oriented
individual, you need to have a well-organized proposal that has
a beginning and an end. An outline with step-by-step clarity
is a good match to what a PROCEDURES person is wanting
to see. Provide evidence (or story) of how your proposal was
used elsewhere, how it was implemented, and what results were
obtained. Be thorough and systematic in your explanation.
Stick to one recommendation. And be certain you include the
end of the process—what the results were and how others felt
about the outcome.

When you encounter resistance, do not add features or
benefits. Stick with your plan. Resistance is most apt to occur when your plan lacks details. Notice when the resistance
occurs and clarify that part of the process. If you encounter
objections that cannot be overcome, you can then say, "There is
one other approach that has been useful for many companies.
May I describe it to you?"

A second approach for selling a PROCEDURES person
is to convince them that the procedure has already begun!
Shelle Rose Charvet (In Words that Change Minds) provides
an excellent application of this technique:

"The first step is, I'll show you how we have laid
out these products. Then you can look at the
merchandise and try it out. After that I'll tell
you about the payment plan and we can choose

which one will fit your needs and set it up for you to sign, and lastly, you can take your product home right away"

With a PROCEDURES person, you may want to use statements such as the following:

"We have found that one way works better than the others."

"Let me walk you through the whole process step-by-step."

"First, you may want to do this. Then,…"

"Because this process has been used so many times, it's reliability is well-established."

"We have what I call a 7-Step Plan. First,…"

"This proven methodology gives you confidence that it can be implemented easily."

EXERCISE

Options / Procedures

1. Describe the benefits of one of your products or services for an OPTIONS person.

2. Describe the benefits of one of your products or services for a PROCEDURES person.

Label the following statements or behaviors as OPTIONS or PROCEDURES:

1. "There must be other approaches."

2. "How do I get out of my current contract?"

3. "How do I get from the initial application to knowing that I am fully covered?"

4. "Suppose I want to split the cost across divisions?"

5. "How many different models are there from which to choose?"

6. "That first step seems very complicated."

ANSWERS

1. O   3. P   5. O

2. P   4. O   6. P

MINDSETS: SAME/DIFFERENT

Think about how you react when told of a new idea? Do you notice how similar it is to past ideas? Or do you quickly see how it is different? If you go to buy a new car, what do you notice: similarities to your old one or differences? What relationship do you see between what you are doing today and what you did in your last job? Do you think about how it is similar or different?

Think about your reaction to this chapter or to the whole book. How would you compare or contrast this approach to selling with how you have worked in the past? Do you note differences or similarities? Do you look for what you can keep in your current style while adding a bit of new approaches? What do you say to yourself as you see new selling suggestions? The answers to these questions can help you understand the next Mindset: SAME/DIFFERENT.

The SAME/DIFFERENT Mindset is sometimes called "Matching/Mismatching" in NLP literature. The idea is the same: you look for how things match what you already know or you look for ways things are mismatched or different.

Although still a MINDSET, the SAME/DIFFERENT Mindset differs from the other Mindsets in one fundamental way. There are actually four levels rather than two extremes and the middle:

- SAME
- Similar with difference or exception
- Different with exceptions
- DIFFERENT

The "with exception" Mindsets are the second thought reactions to a new situation. In other words, some people look for what is SAME and then quickly look at what is different. Similarly, people may look first at how a new thing is DIFFERENT but quickly shift to noticing similarities to the old.

People who demonstrate a strong SAME Mindset probably only constitute about 5% of the population according to Bailey. These are people who really do not like change and hold on tight to what is known and secure in their world. They like consistency. They want safety and stability in their work environment. It is a challenge to get them to change vendors or products at times. If something is working, they do not want to rock the boat.

People who demonstrate a strong DIFFERENT Mindset probably make up about 20% of the U.S. population. They like change, and they can become a challenge in a group by always pointing out problems or potential surprises. They do not look for how a new idea matches what has worked well. They go quickly for the mismatch. These are the type of people who believe that any change is good. It shakes things up. They are quick to criticize the status quo, and they are apt to talk constantly about "thinking outside the box." Can you see why change is difficult in organizations when only 20% of the people are apt to enjoy the process of change?

Roger Bailey's work suggests that as many as 65% of the population is SAME-with-Exception. These people are comfortable with a little change over time, and if given time, they can adapt to change forced on them with a moderate amount of stress.

People who are DIFFERENT-with-Exception make up (according to Bailey) about 10% of the population. They like change, especially if they are the change agents. They will move things around and make minor adjustments on a regular basis. They will rewrite policies and add functions to software programs when they can. They need some change in their lives.

NOTE:

People with a DIFFERENT Mindset can always find the flip-side to an argument. They are the classic, "Yes, but..." individuals. They often have an argument for why something will not work. When presented with an idea, they often respond, "Yes, but there are real problems with this. Have you considered a different approach instead, such as...?" In a team, this can be very helpful discipline for planning, but if used constantly, such habitual verbal behavior can be irritating. People with a DIFFERENT Mindset must learn how to use their helpful perspective without antagonizing others.

WORDS TO NOTICE

People with a SAME Mindset will talk a lot about how things seem to look or feel the same. The like stability, and they seek to reassure themselves by seeing similarities with the past that they liked. They are likely to say such things as the following:

> "This looks a lot like the old model."
> "I'm not sure why your proposal would be an improvement."
> "But I like the way our deliveries are made."
> "I really trust our people. Changing that doesn't make sense."

People with an Exception Mindset will notice gradual change. They will comment that things are "getting better" or "getting worse." They are also likely to say such things as the following:

> "I notice that your ideas are similar to what we have today but you are starting to get at a few ways to improve. Continue."
>
> "This is weird but might actually be helpful. We did something off-the-wall like this once before."
>
> "This is certainly unusual, but my guys often like unusual."

People with a DIFFERENT Mindset enjoy talking about how things could be (or were) different. In addition, they are quick to argue about anything and everything. They are often heard saying things such as the following:

> "No. I want something more creative than this."
>
> "Instead of this, let's try this…"
>
> "I don't see why you would think that would work!"
>
> "Too complicated. Not a chance it would work."

I had a client who was a classic DIFFERENT person. He could accept nothing as it was presented to him. He would pick me up at the airport and always find something to say to mismatch, even if he were late. "I expected you at a different door." "I didn't expect you to be wearing a blue suit."

With his people, everything he said to them was about what they were NOT doing. "She starts her day at this end of the plant instead of that one." "He says this is what he wants to do but it is wrong." He is a sincere individual who wants to treat his people right, but he is incapable of matching and accepting what is given him. He must challenge and counter every comment and behavior. Needless to say, it is a struggle for people who work with him on a daily basis. Yet, his observations are usually sound and valid in the right context. His people learn to work with him by not having any real commitment to their proposed ideas but using them as conversation starters that eventually lead to the CEO explaining what he wants at that moment.

DISCOVERY QUESTIONS

Typical Discovery Questions might be:

- "What is the relationship between business this year and last year?"
- "What are you looking for in a proposal? What needs to be there for you to be happy?"
- "What is the relationship between what you are focusing on this year and your focus in your job last year?"

SELLING HINTS

To help sell a SAME person, it is important to remember that they find comfort in seeing how something is similar to what they have seen done or known in the past. Therefore, you must tell them the areas that are consistent and not changed in what you propose. Use words like, "As you know...", "Like before...", "Identical to your earlier program...", or "Unchanged..."

> "While this is a new product, the key components are very similar to what we used before…"
>
> "Notice that the framework remains unchanged. If something isn't broken, we see no reason to change it for change sake."

With SAME buyers, it is also important to look for and talk about areas of agreement.

> "As you mentioned earlier, you liked this particular feature…"
>
> "I fully agree that we do not want to raise this issue with the executives at this time."
>
> "The worst thing we could do, as you said earlier, is to change the delivery dates that people have relied on…"

With DIFFERENT people, it is good to talk about what is new or different. Use words like "New", "Different", "Improved", "Unique for you", or "State of the art."

> "This is a completely new approach—very different from what has been done in the past."
>
> "We looked at your program and propose changing much of it to be more effective for you."

Although it is risky, with someone who is so DIFFERENT oriented that he/she argues with everything presented, offer an idea that will probably not work and help guide their objections toward what you really want. This is not an easy approach and has the risk of backfiring. Still, with those who love to mismatch and argue, it can be effective.

> "I'm not sure our resources are the best match for you, given that we have quite a dif-

ferent approach than your folks are accustomed to seeing."

"You seem quite happy with the services you are now receiving. I don't want to wreck a good thing for you by proposing something new and different."

"I doubt if you can get your foreman to be willing to try this out on his line."

For people who are the "Exception" people you may want to talk about how things are the same at times and, at other times, how aspects of your proposal are different. This would also be your approach when you have a mixed audience or are unsure of your audience's Mindsets.

"There are some differences here when compared to what you use today—differences that are new and even somewhat revolutionary. However, I also want to point out that the features that have served you well in the past are also present in this program..."

"This is an upgrade—similar to but better than your current equipment. And there is one aspect that is quite unique..."

EXERCISE

Same / Different

1. Describe the benefits of one of your products or services for a SAME person.

2. Describe the benefits of one of your products or services for a DIFFERENT person.

Label the following statements or behaviors as SAME or DIFFERENT:

1. "This sounds much like what I'm doing now."

2. "I think we should go a different direction."

3. "Can I still get it in green?"

4. "That's not going to work."

5. "That's too much change for right now."

6. "I don't see that much difference to justify the price."

MINDSETS: PROACTIVE/REACTIVE

Some people are "starters." They are apt to have a high activity level. They want to get things moving and get other people moving, too. They have an impact on the world around them that is visible. They typically want results that are measurable and meaningful. In NLP terms, these people are called PROACTIVE.

PROACTIVE people want to be busy, but it must be a meaningful busy. There must be an outcome. If a process gets stalled or a meeting drags, PROACTIVE people will get restless. They also will resent having their attempts to initiate action thwarted or criticized by others. They need to feel they can drive the activity level of a group. They sometimes act as if they control the world.

According to Roger Bailey, 15-20%% of the population in the U.S. are in the PROACTIVE group.

REACTIVE people are less obvious in their behaviors. They are less likely to have a visible impact on the people around them. They are inclined to be patient and often more methodical. They need time to think about something before they act. They act most quickly when something forces their hand. They will wait for the phone to ring, for instance, rather than be a "hunter" in the sales world. They often avoid making a commitment and will wait to see how others vote. They need something or someone to which they can react. They may act as if they feel the world controls them.

REACTIVES do not typically initiate an action. They prefer to reflect and think about a situation. They are likely to request a lot of information from you and avoid making a commitment. Sellers can get frustrated with repeated requests for more data and need to learn to ask what data is most relevant. Unlike "Collectors" (another metaprogram) who collect data with no real intention of making a decision, REACTIVE people want to be useful. Often their value is in helping to uncover issues that might be overlooked in a rush to action. They are helpful in a team because of their ability to evaluate information. They are not afraid to make a decision or act. However, they need something to react to to bring them into an action mode. They want understanding before they will make a decision. Finding the data to generate an action is the challenge to someone trying to sell a REACTIVE.

According to Roger Bailey, about 15-20% of the population in the U.S. fall into the REACTIVE group. The remaining population falls into the in-between or BOTH group.

WORDS TO NOTICE

A person who is biased in a PROACTIVE direction is likely to say things such as the following:

> "Lets get moving."
> "Can't we make a decision?
> "We are killing this with too much planning. Let's get started."
> "Just do it."
> "What are we waiting for?"
> "You are good but you're slow."
> "Let's make our own luck"

A person with a REACTIVE Mindset, is likely to say things such as the following:

> "Maybe."
> "I supposed we could. Let me check with my team."
> "I should sleep on this."

"That might work. I'll ask around for what others think."

"Perhaps, but I need time to think about it."

"What do you think?"

"We probably aren't ready for that yet. My guys are likely to resist it."

DISCOVERY QUESTIONS

Typical Discovery Questions might include the following:
- "Think about a recent project you led. How did it get started?"
- "What led to this RFP...was it in response to an issue or something you wanted?"

SELLING HINTS

The PROACTIVE Mindset is oriented toward getting a project started. They often want to start before enough details have been presented. For a sellers, this can lead to early disappointment and surprises. It can also lead to a project being killed because the PROACTIVE may have given approval without checking with enough other people. While a seller loves a PROACTIVE customer, care must be taken to ensure the approval or purchase will not get vetoed later.

With a PROACTIVE Mindset, it can be helpful to ask questions such as the following:

"What do you think we should do now?

"When will we see a result?"

"Where do you want to start?"

"How would you like to start?"

"I doubt that you want to wait on this."

With a REACTIVE Mindset, it is helpful to allow the person time to think but ensure that you are part of the process. Offer to help identify what needs more consideration, and try to include the person's "thinking time" as part of a procedure that is underway and ultimately includes you again. It can be helpful to ask questions like the following:

> "What are people saying?"
> "What happens if we do nothing? "
> "Can we get the job done?"
> "Where do you think most people would like you to start?"
> "As you think about it, what specific issues do you want to analyze more closely?"
> "I certainly do not want to rush your decision; how can I help?"
> "Why don't you think about it until Tuesday, and then we can narrow the choices down."
> "What can I help you understand more thoroughly?"
> "Maybe you are due a little luck?"
> "What part don't you understand enough to feel comfortable?"
> "Once you have equipment installed, you'll understand why…"

For people with BOTH characteristics (or for unknown audiences), use any combination of these type of comments. Remember, most people are in-between PROACTIVE and REACTIVE.

EXERCISE

Proactive / Reactive

1. Describe a benefit of your product or service for a
   PROACTIVE person.

2. Describe a benefit of your product or service for a
   REACTIVE person.

Label the following statements or behaviors as PROACTIVE or REACTIVE:

1. "Let's just do it."

2. "I need time to think about this a bit."

3. "I may wait until we really have a problem."

4. "I say go. Don't worry about my boss."

5. "I'm not ready to commit yet."

ANSWERS

1. P   3. R   5. R

2. R   4. P

MINDSETS: GENERAL/SPECIFIC

In business, you are constantly taking in information and analyzing it. But how much can you handle at one time? How do you like to start?

According to Roger Bailey, 60% of the population in the U.S. like to begin with an overview. They like GENERAL information first. Outlines, concepts, summaries or a clear agenda provide an overview to a situation that most people like. Too much detail can overwhelm a GENERAL person. You may see his/her eyes glaze over when the details are too complete or the story too long. A GENERAL person can be a challenge for a seller, because he/she may not tell the real reason they want to change suppliers or buy a service. The real need or hot button may stay hidden without careful questioning. Sometimes, he/she must be asked, "How will you know, in six months, if you have made the right decision? Can you give me some concrete examples of what you want to see or be able to report?"

SPECIFIC people make up about 15% of the population. They want details and handle information well. They quickly "chunk down" from a generalization to the specifics that make up the overview. They ask lots of questions, and they are most comfortable working a project with sequential steps to follow. They tend to think in a linear fashion with one detail leading to the next. They may not perceive the connections between information, however, and as a result, knowing what detail is more important than another can be a problem. As Joseph O'Connor wrote in Successful Selling with NLP, "They might be found cleaning the life boats while the ship goes down."

To them, the challenge is to go from A to Z. One way to recognize a SPECIFIC person is to notice what they do when their thinking is interrupted. They usually have to go to the beginning and start over.

> **NOTE:**
>
> **When trying to close with a SPECIFIC, it is helpful to repeat in detail what they have said they wanted ("echo mirror") and then lead into your suggestions in a detailed, procedural manner. An implied cause/effect can also work well for some SPECIFICS if you use enough data.**

WORDS TO NOTICE

A person who is biased in a GENERAL direction is likely to say things such as the following:

> "We are on track."
> "We've got a good plan."
> "I expect things to be done right."
> "This should do the trick."
> "I need a solution."
> "The whole thing is messed up."

A person with a SPECIFIC Mindset is likely to say things such as the following:

> "We started about 9:22 but some people didn't get in until close to 9:28."
> "The first step required getting the password. Then we were able to..."
> "I expect the linen to be on the top shelf... the napkins on the second shelf with the table-cloths on the bottom two shelves next to it, and the bar towels..."

DISCOVERY QUESTIONS

Typical Discovery questions might include:

- " What are you working on now? Tell me about it."
- "What would you like most to hear—the overview or the specifics?"

SELLING HINTS

When a buyer has a GENERAL Mindset, it can sometimes be difficult to know what he/she really wants. You must avoid being misled by generalizations. Do not be afraid to ask clarifying questions. In addition, begin your presentation or proposal with an overview or summary that relates to an outcome. Then add details as necessary. You will only know this by watching the buyer carefully. Use phrases such as the following:

"How did you choose your last vendor for this product?"
"The overview is this…"
"Essentially, it looks like this."
"In brief, …"
"The important thing is…"
"I don't want to bore you too many details."

When a prospect or customer has a SPECIFIC Mindset, you must be well-prepared. Come armed with details and supporting information. Walk the customer through the procedure from beginning to end, and use his/her words as much as possible to identify needs you are satisfying with your proposal. Use phrases such as the following:

"First, we are going to do this. Then, next…."

"To be specific, we see exactly…"
"The detailed plan in our proposal is this:…"

For BOTH or with a mixed audience, begin your proposal or presentation with a quick overview or summary and then move quickly into the procedure. However, be aware that those in your audience with a GENERAL Mindset will quickly lose interest if the procedures are too detail. You will want to constantly ask for feedback as to whether you audience wants more or less detail as you progress.

At the beginning of this chapter, you heard five responses to your imaginary proposal. How would you adjust…now that you know MINDSETS?

1. "I don't know. I'm concerned about the problems in that division already."
2. "What other choices are there? Is this the only way you think will work?"
3. "Who else has done this? What was their experience like?"
4. "How do you propose we actually start and what is the specific plan?"
5. "Hmm. I think we should try something different. Suppose we…"

EXERCISE

General / Specific

1. Describe the benefits of one of your products or services for a GENERAL person.

2. Describe the benefits of one of your products or services for a SPECIFIC person.

Label the following statements or behaviors as GENERAL or SPECIFIC.

1. "We are talking about 'change', right?"

2. "Where do you get that cost number? "

3. "Could you spare the details. I don't have all day."

4. "I'm looking to have a real impact."

5. "You aren't telling me anything but generalities."

6. "Wait a minute. Let's back up a bit. I think you skipped a few steps."

13 *Handling Objections Without Losing Rapport*

INTRODUCTION

E veryone hears objections. When you are a seller, objections are part of the process. An objection can either teach you something and provide insights into your prospect, or it can cost you money if mishandled. How you respond, what you say, and even your posture can add to your problem or give you an advantage.

Sometimes, people see an objection as a challenge, an opportunity to debate or negotiate. If you believe an objection is something to be *overcome*, you may find yourself wrestling instead of learning and selling. Often, when a seller views an objection as a negative, that process becomes uncomfortable. The seller may actually fear an objection. Or worse, some sellers are talking to themselves and anticipating an objection: *"I know he is going to complain about our price. I just know it."* Needless to say, such an attitude is distracting and non-productive.

Instead, consider an objection to be a sign that your customer is interested enough in what you are selling to want to learn more. If she thinks your price is too high, you have an opportunity to explore her frame of reference and talk about how well she understands *why* your price seems high to her. It

212

is an opportunity to learn and educate. It is also another time to *sell* rather than *tell*.

NOTE:

Most objections fall into five categories.
It is important for you, if possible, to learn to see which category applies to what your prospect said to you and build your response using that insight. Most objections are based on one of the following realities:

1. **The value of your product/service is not seen.**
2. **The prospect is not in a hurry to make a change.**
3. **There is no money available.**
4. **There is a competitor involved.**
5. **The safe decision is no decision.**

BE CURIOUS

If you stay curious rather than defensive, you will find objections much easier to handle. Ask questions, especially those designed to clarify vague words. **Ask permission** to ask questions, however. Otherwise, you will sound defensive.

> *"If you don't mind my asking, you see our price is high compared to what, specifically?"*
> *"If I may ask, what conditions would have to exist before this decision could be given a higher level of urgency?"*

*"If you don't mind my asking, are you say-
ing there is no money right now, this quarter,
or longer?"*
*"If you don't mind my asking, who else has
been bidding on this project?"*

BE PRESENT

An objection from a customer can often trigger voices in
your head telling you what to say and what not to say. It is not
uncommon that by the time a customer has finished asking
a question or making a statement, you are already thinking
about a response. In fact, sometimes you may assume he/she
knows what is about to be said and jump ahead.

*"I know what you are about to say. You think
the price is too high, right?"*
*"I'm sure we could do more testing. Our lab
could get started right away."*

Unfortunately, this creates two new problems. First, if you
are mind-reading, you are probably wrong. You may even end
up raising a problem that the customer had not even considered.

*"I think if you could order today, our delivery
problems will not impact you at all."*
*"You know we all buy from the same suppli-
er, so you probably are wondering why our price
is higher."*
*"You want a better price? OK, I can probably
drop the shipping charges."*

The real problem with mind-reading and thinking about
your response while someone is talking is even bigger than

what you see in these two examples. The real problem is that you are not being "present." In other words, you are not paying attention to your customer. You might as well be sending a text message to your buddy at the ball park. If you are not concentrating on what the customer is saying, you are not being "present", and you are not being real. You cannot sell YOU if you are not genuine and present. And you cannot sell anything if you are not selling YOU.

NOTE:

Try a simple exercise. Listen to someone telling you about a trip he/she took or a movie recently seen. As the person is talking, make a mark on a piece of paper every time your mind wanders. In other words, every time you think of something else or say something to yourself rather than listen to the speaker, mark a little tally mark on the paper. You will be amazed at how hard it is to listen actively to someone and how fast those tallies add up. It is a skill that takes a lot of practice. Very few people can do it well.

PACE

Once you can stay present and listen, the next challenge is to move from the objection toward a response that clarifies, educates, or moves the discussion in a positive direction. This requires three skills: the ability to **pace, link,** and **lead.**

Pacing is the ability to accept what the person has said. You may not fully agree with the objection, but you do not openly disagree either. You accept the statement in a way that suggests you understand how the prospect could say such a thing.

The key to pacing is paying enough attention to be able to restate what the person has said. Do not generalize. Try to be as specific as you can about what was said and not what you thought it meant. If the words are vague (e.g., *"too high"*, *"not competitive"*, *"You don't understand our problem"*, *etc.*) then take the time to ask questions such as *"If you don't mind my asking, what specifically do I need to understand to be helpful to you?"*.

Once you feel you understand what the person is saying, then PACE.

"I can see why you might say our prices are high."

"Based on your recent experience, I certainly can see why you would say our quality is suspect."

"I know it is hard to change vendors, and I can see why you might not want to go through the hassle."

"You are right. Our price is high."

"That's true."

"I agree."

"I can see why you might say that."

Pacing is the ability to validate what the prospect has said by accepting his or her position and perception. Remember, all reality is perception, and you want to be clear that you are not arguing with the customer's perception at that point in time. By pacing an objection, you are announcing that you respect what the prospect has said. You are also verbally matching the content that was spoken. Both skills are ways of maintaining trust and rapport. By Pacing, you are able to accept an objection and still sell YOU.

Another important part of Pacing is your posture. Carefully mirror your prospect as you state a Pacing response. This helps maintain rapport and reduces the feeling that you are about to lay the groundwork for a debate. By mirroring, you are also increasing the level of attention that you are paying to your prospect which improves your ability to be "present."

EXERCISE

Handling Objections

List at least five of the most common objections you get in your business.

1.

2.

3.

4.

5.

EXERCISE

Handling Objections

Now, write a PACE response to each. Remember, accept what has been said. Re-state the objection and make it clear that you are not arguing.

1.

2.

3.

4.

5.

If you look at your responses in the last exercise, you will see that your comments are probably begging for the next word:

"*Yes, our prices are high. BUT...*"

That is right. **BUT**. Or you may have preferred "however", "yet", "nevertheless", or a host of other words that are really just "but" in disguise.

When you use a "but word", you lose all the power of Pacing. The brain hears the word "but", and it cancels out a conscious awareness of whatever preceded it. You lose the advantage of Pacing when you say, "but." You are no longer building rapport; you will be seen as arguing.

LINK

Instead, you must find a way to **Link** your agreement with the next step, the ability to Lead. The easiest way to do this is to use the word, **AND,** or you can use any of the following:

> *So*
> *While*
> *Therefore*
> *And that means we need to*
> *Which makes it important that*

These are all ways of avoiding any word that resembles "but." You accept the objection, and you are ready to move forward.

Go back and look at your responses in the last exercise. At the end of each response, add the word "and" or one of the equivalent words or phrases. Do not worry about what comes next. Just get used to hearing yourself say, "and" after a Pacing comment.

VAK "BRIDGE"

Once you have accepted the objection by Pacing, your goal is to move quickly away from the objection toward a positive action to clarify and resolve the objection. This is an excellent opportunity to apply the skills from Chapter 5 that relate to VAK matching. As you begin to guide the prospect away from the objection, choose words that match the VAK preference revealed in the objection. Matching can help you quickly lay the groundwork for a productive discussion. VAK matching, like posture mirroring, is a way to strengthen rapport at a time when it can be severely tested. Think of VAK Matching as a "bridge" between what has been said and what you usually say in response. If you can add a simple VAK match between what the prospect said and what you want to say, you have given yourself an advantage.

"Your prices look too high." "I can see why you might say that...."

"I don't want that much material. I need smaller batches." "These loads probably feel pretty cumbersome... "

"Acme says they can beat your price." "I'm not surprised. Can we talk about that a moment?"

LEAD

You have now heard the objection, Paced and Linked the objection and started your response with a VAK match to the prospect's language used in the objection. Your next goal is to get away from the objection and Lead toward a shared action that will resolve the concern. Keep in mind: there are only five likely reasons for an objection. Help the prospect find a solution.

Ask permission to join with the prospect in looking at some information (V), talking about some possibilities (A), or working on some ideas (K) *together*. The key to Leading is to engage the prospect in a shared action to resolve the problems. This must be by invitation, however. Invite the prospect by asking permission or making a suggestion. Do not tell.

"I can see why you might say that, and if you don't mind, I'd like for us to discuss for a moment what is included in that price and how it may not be as high in the long run as it feels right now. Would that be OK?"

"These loads probably feel pretty cumbersome. If you will let me, can I give you some ideas that others have told us about where they were able to handle these bulkier barrels that let them get the price advantage without a hassle?"

"I'm not surprised. Can we talk about that a moment? I'd like to ask you some questions about what you look for in an invoice to make sure that hidden costs don't get buried. Would that be OK?"

The Lead step is also a good opportunity to use VAK Mixing. Use the matching skill initially, and then expand your invitation-to-act with a VAK mix. Notice in the examples above how each statement contains a VAK mix.

FINAL THOUGHTS

The key to handling objections without losing rapport is to keep selling YOU. Avoid arguing and lead the prospect into a problem-solving action. Get permission, mirror, and join forces in solving the problem. And most important: Listen. Few people have ever "listened" their way out of a sale, but many have "talked" their way out of a sale. Listen. Stay present. Pace, Link, and Lead. Keep the advantage.

14 *Keeping the Advantage*

"Don't let it end like this. Tell them I said something."
—Last words of Pancho Villa as quoted by Michael Moncur.

INTRODUCTION

The Unfair Advantage is all about selling YOU! You become the catalyst for creating activity and getting results. You build the rapport. You sell yourself. You earn the advantage.

What happens, then, when you or your prospect leave? What happens when your customer is no longer in front of you or on the phone? That is the challenge of keeping the advantage.

> *Two training specialists in Milwaukee were presenting their ideas to a prospect. In the course of the discussion, the prospect mentioned that her needs were fairly standard with only a few special exceptions. The trainer said, "You mean you want a good old Mom-and-apple-pie type program."*
>
> *"No," she said, "not really. More like chocolate cake."*

223

*They all had a good laugh and continued work-
ing on a program. When the meeting was over and
the prospect was about to leave, one of the trainers
handed her a box. She opened it and discovered a
chocolate cake inscribed with the words, "We listen
to our clients."*

The chocolate cake was a perfect example of matching the client's metaphor. But it was much more than that because she took it home. By linking the day's interaction and positive relationship with the take-home cake, the trainers kept their advantage beyond the walls of the office.

The challenge of keeping the advantage is getting the client to take YOU home. The secret is to find a way to link you to something that will recreate in the prospect's mind the power of your relationship. Since you cannot be there, you need to link YOU to a situation and behavior in the future. In NLP terms, this is called "future pacing." The training specialists in the story above can be confident that when the prospect eats the cake and sees the words "We listen to our clients", the good feelings from the meeting will be relived.

The three ways to keep the advantage are:

1. Playback the experience.

2. Rehearse responses to potential challenges (future pace).

3. Personalize any handouts to help the prospect re-member YOU.

PLAYBACK THE EXPERIENCE

When you have been successful with a prospect, you have obtained a commitment to action—either to buy, recommend, or whatever your objective was. Before you let the person leave you, "rerun" the experience. Guide prospects through a sensory tour of why they will be glad they made today's decision. Help them see, hear, and feel positive aspects of their decision.

> *"We worked a long time to put this deal together. When did you feel it was the right thing to do? What did you see that told you this was going to happen? I hope you are as excited as I am."*
>
> *"You were not sure about this until you saw one key benefit to you. Do you remember what you said? Why do you think that was the tipping point for you?"*
>
> *"This afternoon, you looked at a lot of houses. But I could hear in your voice when you found the right one for you. Do you remember what you said to yourself? What did you see first that made you know you had found your next home?*

If you notice the customer or client is not comfortable answering your questions, you have not completed the sale. Go back to the selling cycle, re-sell, and then rehearse again.

FUTURE PACING

You know that some buyer's remorse occurs in most purchases. People began to second-guess their decisions. Consultants have told me, *"Don't count on the project until the check clears."* Perhaps. Or perhaps it was not sold well the first time.

You can help reduce buyer remorse by rehearsing some of the moments when such doubt may occur. Your success will depend on how well you can anticipate specific doubts or challenges and then guide your client through a response. Be sure to include embedded messages in that rehearsal.

Try to help the person anticipate at least two likely challenges—internal or external. Don't forget peers, competitors, family members, or the person's own personal doubts.

> *"You made a great deal today. Can't you see yourself reaching for that new phone while you are stuck in traffic? You will be very happy you bought this car phone, especially at this price."*
>
> *"What a beautiful home you just bought! What will be the first thing you tell your friends tonight? What will they get most excited about?"*
>
> *"What is Mr. Jones going to say? Wow, really!? Then how will you express your excitement about this project? What will convince him? What can we show him or have ready to tell him when he questions you?"*
>
> *"You know, you are going to get a call in the next few days from XYZ company, and they will try to tell you how much better their deal would be. What are you going to say to yourself when that happens? Are you going to be able to see the holes in their argument? How can I help you remember how good you feel about this right now?"*
>
> *"You know people will challenge you on this. What will help you remember the reasons you made this decision? What do you think is the strongest reason? As you discuss your decision, you may want to remember to tell about..."*

PERSONALIZE THE HANDOUT

Finally, look for a tangible way for the client or prospect to take you home. This is a particularly important element for

NOTE:

One trick to future pacing is to think of it as two statements. The first is something that you know will occur (pace):

"Tomorrow, Joe is going to ask you..."
"When you start getting called by competitors, you are going to begin to ask yourself..."

The second statement is what you want the person to do that helps reinforce the decision (lead):

"Remember how excited you were when you realized..."
"Look at the brochure to see where we marked..."

The trick to using the two statements effectively is to link them with the word AND. Ignore whether there is really a logical sequence. Simply link them:

"Tomorrow, Joe is going to ask you... AND remember how excited you were when ..."
"When you start getting called by competitors, you are going to begin to ask yourself questions...AND look at the brochure to see where we marked AND it will remind you how excited you are about..."

telemarketers who may be asked to "*send me a brochure.*" An anniversary calendar, a company brochure, or the yearly catalog are not substitutes for YOU. They can be helpful, however. The secret is to link YOU to the product. Find a way to personalize that tangible product to trigger a recall of you and the rapport you enjoyed when interacting.

• Business Card

The easiest example of a trigger can be found with the business card. Never just hand it out. Typically, business cards are exchanged before rapport has been established. That is the established pattern. However, before you leave, take it back and add your home phone number on the back. Or at the very least, take it back and underline your extension. As you do so, add a verbal embedded message such as "*You are not going to do business with Acme, you are going to work with me personally. And here is how to reach me directly.*" The combination of an embedded message and your physically marking the card will help create a trigger to link YOU to that card.

> *One of the best examples I have seen of how to use a business card to keep the advantage was from a gentleman who runs a commercial trucking business. His business card, to the casual observer, looks like any ordinary card. However, he starts to hand it to you and then abruptly pulls it back. He then carefully folds it in half. The result is a picture of the back of one of his trucks. The folded ends of the card become the doors of the truck. When you open the "doors", the card information is revealed. No ordinary card and no ordinary salesman.*

NOTE:

The more you can create a full VAK scenario with your business card, the more powerful it can be: *"Larry, in a couple of weeks, you may be going crazy with end-of-the-month problems. When that happens, look out your window, remember this card, and call TempFolks. It's on the card you hold in your hand. My number is on it. Call me and I will bring the troops."* Make your card a living extension of YOU.

• Catalogues and Brochures

When you send a catalogue to a customer, it is important that you "future pace" the prospect's behavior. You can do this by personalizing the brochure and then leading with embedded messages. Pace and lead the behavior and help guide the prospect to do what you want done.

> *"I am sending you our new catalog. I have marked two pages that you will have special interest in...page 4 and page 5. When you get the catalog, look at page 4 and you will see what I am telling you. I think you will get excited by what you see... Then give me a call..."*

SUMMARY

The key to keeping the advantage is to keep alive the relationship you have enjoyed with the customer or prospect. Make certain they take YOU home. Practice what you will say and do to Keep the Advantage:

1. **What do you want?**
2. **How will you increase or strengthen your client's commitment?**
3. **What should you rehearse?**
4. **What command(s) will be embedded?**
5. **How do you provide YOU as a take-along?**

![ ]

EXERCISE

Keeping the Advantage

You have just sold your service or product. Congratulate your customer/client on the decision. Create a full sensory experience, using all three language preferences.

However, you know your customer tends to continue to look at prices of your competitors after a purchase decision has been made, whether it be a new car, a new suit, an airplane lease, or a punch press. Rehearse "What if..." scenarios. Include "*Do you have what you need to recall your reasons for this decision, to remind you why you feel good now about your decision and you want others to have the same feeling?*" Use your own words and include a VAK mix and some embedded messages such as "*feel good about your decision.*"

Keeping The Advantage Exercise:
Sample Answers

You have just sold your service or product. Congratulate your customer/client on the decision. Create a full sensory experience, using all three language preferences.

"Jim, you have made a great choice with this model. You've listened to it here, but when you see it at home, you will be wild. You'll have to call your friend Ray and show it to him—what do you think he'll say when he sees it? Will he be excited like you are?"

You know your customer tends to continue to look at prices of your competitors after a purchase decision has been made, whether it be a new car, a new suit, an airplane lease, or a punch press. Rehearse "What if..." scenarios. Include *"Do you have what you need to recall your reasons for this decision, to remind you why you feel good now about your decision and you want others to have the same feeling?"* Use your own words and include a VAK mix and some embedded messages such as *"feel good about your decision."*

"Sue, we both know there are lots of insurance companies who would like your business. You have made a wise choice and you've seen the information that helped you make that decision. Do you have enough ammunition to take home to explain to others, like Fred, why this was the right choice? You feel good about this decision, and I want to give you enough support material to help you make Fred and others see that it was the best decision. I'll mark this page, here, which is where you and I realized that this was the right choice for you because... This mark will help you remember what we said."

Special Application: Presentations/ Team Selling

15

INTRODUCTION

Formal presentations and team selling offer a unique opportunity to use many of the techniques of The Unfair Advantage. Non-verbal pacing, embedded commands, and ideas for keeping the advantage are all applicable to team selling. In addition, if only one person speaks, the other members of the team can observe and use those observations to increase your effectiveness.

PREPARING THE PRESENTATION

Clarify your specific goals for each segment (What are you trying to accomplish today?) and construct your action commands. Embed them carefully in your opening statements.

Carefully plan the opening statements for each speaker. Remember, each speaker must establish rapport with the audience. Identify what you know about your audience. If you know nothing, include a rich VAK mix in your opening. However, if you know something about the key decision makers, use that information. (*We had a client who used tapes of their client from television interviews to determine language preference!*) If you know your client has certain metaphors that

233

are part of the working vocabulary, you may want to insert the metaphor into your opening remarks. Consider including enough client-specific jargon following the VAK mix to help your credibility.

Finally, prepare your handouts and take-home materials. Decide when you will distribute the handouts. Remember: you cannot compete with the handouts. Time their release carefully. Once handed out, remember to take the time to guide people through each page. Such guidance is a powerful form of pacing and rapport-building. Then decide how to personalize the take-home materials. Be sure your personal fingerprint is on whatever is left behind.

PRESENTING

Prior to your speaking, try to meet the key people in your audience. Pace each non-verbally. Even if you are seated, pace each person until it is time for you to speak.

When it is time to present, be sensitive to the mood of the group as a whole. That mood must be paced when you begin your presentation. If the group is energetic and jovial, begin your opening comments with such energy. If the mood is reserved, match that mood. Pace the group. Do not make the mistake of trying to liven up a dead room by being the life of the party. You need to pace first and then lead.

The first speaker should begin with the prepared opening that includes a VAK mix. After the opening, be flexible. If for some reason you are not connecting with your audience, be prepared to try something different. For instance, if your audience is not listening to you, hand out your support material immediately. Guide them through the handouts as a way of pacing and building rapport. Then gradually ease them away from the material back to watching and listening to you. Some audiences are more Auditory than others. Some are Visual or Kinesthetic. If you notice no one is looking at your slides, forget them and try either more discussion or more reference to handouts. You may overcome audience inattention by asking questions of key people, *if* the key people are Auditory. (This will also help give you an opportunity to mirror individuals more intently and, hopefully, engage in useful dialogue.) Let your audience guide your presentation. Keep your presentation plan flexible at all times. Be prepared to present your ideas in all three languages, and then let your audience guide you.

Remember, when you use slides or overheads, you are competing with those for attention. The competition is especially brutal if your audience is more Visual than Auditory. Consequently, never speak over a slide. Also, be certain that the lighting emphasizes you and not the slide. Never present in the dark for the sake of a slide. It is better to have the slide a little washed-out from too much room light than to have you in the dark. You cannot establish rapport if no one can see you.

When you show a slide, turn toward the screen as if you are now a member of the audience, and either read it or point out the key points on the slide. Be an audience member at that moment. Pace the audience. Then, when you are through with the slide, turn it off. It is also helpful to physically make a hand motion to guide the audience's eyes from the screen back to you.

Finally, try to avoid having any topic last more than forty-five minutes without a break of some kind. Kinesthetics, particularly, need a chance to squirm and even stand up. Auditories also get tired of intently listening. Forty-five minutes is about as long as you dare go without some kind of interruption to break the pattern.

TEAMWORK

If you are part of a team making a presentation, your team members should be carefully mirroring your client while you are speaking. You may assign team members to specific client participants or just have everybody mirror each person over the course of the presentation. No team member should be idle at any point. Each should either be speaking or mirroring a client.

As you speak and interact, one of your team members may notice that some people in the audience respond more readily to visual stimuli, for instance, than to your speaking. If that occurs, your teammate should clue you, especially if you are not connecting with the key decision-maker. For instance, if the key decision-maker intently stares at a slide but drifts away once you turn off the projector, your team member may clue you as you speak by saying, "Tim, I'm not sure everyone could see what you were getting at right there. Can you clarify it a bit?" The key word—"see"—clues you, the speaker, to use more Visual words at that moment.

One critical problem with team selling is the "hand-off." You may have built good rapport with your client, but now it is time for someone else to speak. You can help the transfer by inviting the next speaker to join you briefly in front of the audience. This process helps link you with the next presenter. Give a short introduction of your teammate, and then sit down. However, once you are seated, actively mirror the key people to help transfer the rapport you have built.

KEEP THE ADVANTAGE

Finally, remember the lessons from Chapter 14. Use the handouts to help leave YOU behind. During the presentation, "teach" your client how to use the handouts. Show them what to remember and when. Play back key moments in the presentation and link to the handouts. Remember it is YOU, not the handouts, that is the advantage.

16 Special Application: Letters/Memo Writing

INTRODUCTION

L etter writing is an ideal opportunity to use The Unfair Advantage. It provides time to think about what message you are sending and to engineer it well. The process of writing a good sales or marketing letter has three steps:

1. Write down your initial ideas.

Do not worry about form. Concentrate on the key ideas you want in that letter. If possible, begin with a reference to the last interaction you had as a way of "keeping the advantage."

2. Edit to provide a good mix of VAK words.

You want to add richness and balance to your letter. You also do not know the reader's preferred language, and you want to ensure that you match his language as early as possible. Therefore, an early mix is important. Do not try to change the content. Merely enrich the packaging.

3. Embed the appropriate commands.

Remember—you must say what you want. Decide on the key commands and find ways to embed them.

The following letters are examples of applying this process to a proposal letter.

DRAFT ONE:

Dear Jim:

It was good to see you again last Wednesday. I am glad you found the NLP introduction to be interesting and useful.

As you requested, I am writing to propose two half-day programs for you—one each for your two groups of telemarketing people. The programs would be similar to the one you already saw. They will probably include some new things to give it a slightly different look, however. There will definitely be more practice time.

The objectives of the two programs should be similar to what you have seen. Since both groups are largely dealing with customers through phone contacts or by mail, we can focus on these areas: getting leads, qualifying leads, and obtaining add-on sales. We will also look at how to resolve customer complaints and reduce customer hostility.

When we are done, your people will have several new ideas for verbal scripts as well as techniques for responding more effectively to customers.

Jim, I hope this gives you some ideas. I am looking forward to working with you and your telemarketing groups.

Sincerely,

Duane Lakin, Ph.D.
Management Psychologist

Can you SEE the problem with this letter? As I concentrated on what I wanted to say, I allowed my visual preference to show. In addition, there are few action commands.

DRAFT TWO: (Note the changes in bold print.)

Dear Jim:

It was good to see you again last Wednesday. I was glad to hear you found the NLP introduction interesting and useful.

As you requested, I am writing to propose two half-day programs for you—one each for your two groups of telemarketing people. The programs would look about the same as the one for your management group, except I would talk about some new ideas that would be unique to telemarketing. I would add some things to give it a little different feel. There will definitely be more practice time.

The objectives of the two programs should be similar to what you have seen. Since both groups are largely dealing with customers through phone contacts or by mail, we can focus on these areas: getting leads, qualifying leads, and obtaining add-on sales. We will also talk about how to resolve customer complaints and reduce customer hostility.

When we are done, your people will have several new ideas for verbal scripts as well as techniques for responding more effectively to customers. In addition, participants should have a better feel for their role as service professionals <u>and</u> selling professionals.

Jim, I hope this gives you some ideas. You have seen the basic program, and you have a good sense for the potential contribution it can make. I am looking forward to working with you and your telemarketing group, and I will call you on the 28th to find out how this sounds to you.

Sincerely,
Duane Lakin, Ph.D.
Management Psychologist

The second draft of the letter has a better VAK balance. Yet it still lacks punch. There are too few action commands.

DRAFT THREE: (Note the embedded messages are bold and major changes from Draft Two are ~~lined out~~.)

Dear Jim:

It was good to see you again last Wednesday. I am glad to hear you ~~found the NLP introduction interesting and useful.~~ continue to find The Unfair Advantage interesting and useful.

As you requested, I am writing to ~~propose~~ suggest you choose two half-day programs—one each for your two groups of telemarketing people. The programs would look about the same as the one for your management group, except I would talk about some new ideas that would be unique to telemarketing. I would add some things to give it a little different feel. There will definitely be more practice time to help them believe in the power of The Unfair Advantage.

The objectives of the two programs should be similar to what you have seen. Since both groups are largely dealing with customers through phone contacts or by mail, we can focus on these areas: getting leads, qualifying leads, and obtaining add-on sales. We will also talk about how to resolve customer complaints and reduce customer hostility.

~~When we are done, your people will have several new ideas for verbal scripts as well as techniques for responding more effectively to customers.~~ If we can help them buy The Unfair Advantage and use it every day, your people will have several new ideas for responding more effectively to customers. In addition, participants should have a better feel for their role as service professionals <u>and</u> selling professionals.

Jim, I hope this gives you some ideas. You have seen the basic program, and you have a good sense for the potential contribution it can make. ~~I am looking forward to working with you and your telemakreting group.~~ You know best if your people need The Unfair Advantage. I look forward to our working together, and I will call you on the 28th to find out ~~how this sounds to you~~ if this proposal sounds like what you need.

Sincerely,
Duane E. Lakin, Ph.D.
Management Psychologist

The finished letter now contains:

1. Reference to our past (positive) interaction
2. VAK mix
3. Embedded commands

The letter has The Unfair Advantage.

17 *Special Application: Telemarketing*

TEN SECOND MOMENT-OF-TRUTH

The advantage in telemarketing belongs to the caller who can establish rapport and lead the prospect or customer. Yet every telemarketer (TSR, CSR) knows how hard it is to gain and maintain rapport on the phone.

In a face-to-face encounter, you often have several minutes to establish rapport. On the phone, you have only a few seconds to establish enough rapport to keep the person on the line. We sometimes call this the "Ten-second moment of truth." In those ten seconds, you control whether your call will be a success or a failure.

SELECTION ISSUES

Not everyone can be successful on the phone. Our research has indicated that the two biggest factors for predicting success in telemarketing are *FLEXIBILITY* and *LOCUS OF CONTROL*. Flexibility refers to the ability to listen and adapt to the prospect or customer. A characteristic psychologists call "locus of control" refers to a person's belief that personal persistence and determination are what makes one "lucky." In other words, "the harder I work, the luckier I get." These two factors are critical in selecting successful TSRs and CSRs.

243

Both of the key factors can be assessed prior to hiring. First, for assessing "locus of control", we have found success with some of the screening instruments on the market. Whichever test you use, it must be customized to fit your work setting. For instance, we discovered one published test correctly identified the best people for our clients in Winnipeg and Chicago. However, the test had to be significantly modified to fit the people working in a call center in Johnson City, Tennessee. With some refinement, "Locus of Control" and other factors such as maturity and persistence can be successfully assessed with a validated testing program.

Flexibility is a little harder to evaluate. With many of our clients, we test this in a role-playing exercise like an actor's audition. First, the candidate reads a script. Then he/she is told to read it again, this time in a boring, unexciting manner. Then the candidate is asked to read it as if it were the single most exciting thing in the world. If the candidate can follow these instructions, he or she can be taught to listen and can respond to direction. If the candidate *cannot* read the script in three different ways, what will he/she do when a supervisor says, "*You need to sound more enthusiastic*"? If people cannot hear the difference in a role-playing exercise, they probably cannot monitor their own performance or hear the different vocal cues from their customers. The lack of flexibility indicated by the inability to follow such directions interferes with training and delivery of any script or message.

Obviously, factors such as diction, drive, empathy, integrity, maturity, self-discipline and enthusiasm are important factors, too. Fortunately, a combination of interviewing, testing, and role-playing can help measure these attributes and substantially improve the quality of the people you hire.

SCRIPT ENGINEERING

Once you have hired good people, give them good tools with which to work. The best tool is a good script. A good script must be one that helps personalize the interaction and create rapport. It also must be one that helps lead the caller in the desired direction. In customer service calls, for instance, this means focusing the other person on problem solving. In outbound sales calls, the initial "desired direction" simply means keeping the person on the phone, and then leading toward a decision to buy what you are selling. These objectives are not going to be met by saying, "*Hello. My name is Fred Brown, and I am calling on behalf of MergerMania. How are you this evening?*"

A well-engineered script for outbound telemarketing must contain the following basic elements:

1. Clear objectives
2. Embedded messages
3. Initial differentiation of caller from company
4. VAK mixing for impact

Any time you use an embedded message, you must be very clear about your objective. What exactly do you want your prospect to do? Is that outcome possible immediately or are interim objectives needed?

In the case of most telemarketing calls, your objective is to get the "invitation" to continue the presentation. The invitation is achieved by convincing the prospects to talk with you. If they hang up or refuse to interact with you, you cannot get the invitation. You must get the prospect to talk to you. That is the primary initial objective for any outbound call. Therefore, an engineered script often sounds like this:

*"Hello. I'm Fred Brown, and MergerMania has asked me to **talk** to you to help you see how you can save money on your phone bills. I only need to **talk** with you about 3 minutes for you to decide if we can save you money. Is this a good time to **talk** to me?"*

This sample script has three components:

- Primary embedded message: **talk, talk to me**
- Secondary embedded messages: **save money**
- Immediate VAK Mix: **talk, see, save** (AVK)

By repeating "talk", you greatly increase the chances of the prospect saying "*Yes*" to "*...Is this a good time...?*" (The delivery of these lines is critical and discussed below.)

Another aspect of the opening is the differentiation of the caller (Fred Brown) and the company (MergerMania). People are less likely to be rude to a person than to a company. While it probably seems like a small detail, the message "*The company has asked me to talk to you*" invites a relationship between two people.

NOTE:

As the presentation advances, the distinction between the person and the company needs to be eliminated. Eventually, "Fred Brown" disappears and the script begins to refer to "We" and MergerMania, but the invitation stage requires a person-to-person exchange. This relationship is also encouraged by the final question, "Is this a good time to talk to *me*?"

In one campaign, sales increased 30% by simply introducing an opening script similar to this one! In another, sales increased 18% when we changed just the first sentence of the script to read like the one above. The power of engineering simple words is obvious.

After the prospect has given you the invitation to continue (*"Yes, go ahead"* or *"I guess"*), the script needs an immediate VAK mix and an immediate embedded message to tell what you want the person to do next:

> *It must make you **angry** when you **see** other phone rates are lower than yours. Have you **heard** that if you **want MergerMania**, you only pay 7 cents for a minute. Do you know what you pay now?*

Important components of this second script are the following:

- VAK mix: **angry** (K), **see** (V), and **heard** (A)
- Embedded message: **want MergerMania**

The VAK mix ensures two things. First, you know you have matched the preferred language of the prospect, since you have used all three language options. Second, you have also increased the chances of arousing interest by appealing to and stimulating all three senses (visual, auditory, and kinesthetic). You have begun to establish rapport and you have begun to stimulate subliminal interest.

The new embedded message serves to attach the stimulated interest to a decision or choice: **want MergerMania**. In a sense, it is a form of what some people call a "trial-close." In the next part of your script and in any unscripted interactions, you will want to include the phrase **want MergerMania** as often as possible to reinforce the message:

*"We **want MergerMania** to help reduce your phone bill..."*

*"To help you decide you **want MergerMania**, let me tell you about..."*

*"We **want MergerMania** to make it easy for you to save money..."*

Depending on your product or service, you may decide to push more aggressively for a close. In that case, a new embedded message should be introduced as soon as possible:

*"When people **sign up with MergerMania**, they see..."*

*"Before you might decide to **sign up with MergerMania**, let me tell you what others have said..."*

*"Have you seen our '**sign up with MergerMania**' ads on the television?...remember when..."*

*"Once you **sign up with MergerMania**, you will start getting..."*

EXERCISE

Script Writing

You are responsible for selling Widget-On, a home cleaning treatment that will solve the common problem of *shagfonz* in the home. (*Shagfonz* allegedly causes sick house plants, finicky cats, premature hair loss in men, and antisocial adolescent behavior.) American Widgets has discovered a low cost way to treat *shagfonz*. You need an opening script to gain an invitation to continue, a follow-up script with a strong VAK mix, and an embedded message for the actual presentation.

Examples of a possible script:

"Hello. My name is Jan Oaks. Widget-On, the company that found a cure for shagfonz, has asked me to talk with you for a moment. I'd like to talk to you about this discovery. Is this a good time to talk or would you rather talk to me another time?" (Embedded *"talk"*)

... *"You've probably seen our ads on TV. Widget-On has found how to solve the problem of shagfonz. When you use Widget-On, you'll see that what you've heard about us is true. We are very proud of this discovery. Let me ask you..."* (VKKVAKA)

SCRIPT ADJUSTMENTS

As you begin using a script, it is not unusual to notice hang-ups occur at the same place in the presentation. When this happens, a script adjustment can be made to bridge whatever gap exists and solve the problem.

For instance, a campaign to sell cellular phones was losing prospects early in the call. They would hang up when the TSR tried to get prospects to estimate their likely level of cellular phone usage. (Such information was important for determining which package to offer.)

However, prospects could not or would not answer the questions. We simply added a transition question using a VAK predicate mix: *"If you had an XYZ phone, how do you see yourself deciding to use it...when would you most likely talk to someone?"* The mixed use of Visual ("see"), Auditory ("talk"), and Kinesthetic ("use") predicates increased the likelihood that the prospect would relate to the question and respond. The transition phrase solved the hangup problem!

A similar poblem existed in a credit card campaign. Prospects were hanging up when they had to wait for a supervisor to approve the transaction. This problem was eliminated by reestablishing the caller as a person and differentiating him/her from the problem:

> *"Because a credit card has legal implications, the law requires for your protection that you validate all this information with a supervisor. I have asked her to come over here, but she is a bit busy today. Please be patient with me for another moment. I'm sorry for the delay. I think she is going to be able to help us in just a second...*

This change kept the customer on the phone and solved the problem.

250

SCRIPT DELIVERY ISSUES

The delivery of an engineered script is an important issue. It *cannot* be read like a standard solicitation. It is different and must be delivered in a different manner.

Many of the scripts used today do not require much attention from the caller. It is possible (and, in fact, common) for a caller to deliver a script without thinking about what is being said or how it is being said. Experienced TSRs can change from one campaign to another without much effort, because the scripts tend to sound alike. They substitute new names, but the script is basically the same sing-song "I am calling on behalf of..." script. Such scripts lack impact and make relationship-building almost impossible.

CONTROLLED PHRASING

An engineered script demands an active involvement of the caller. He/she must think about what is being said and how to deliver it. Phrasing and breathing are disciplined and controlled by the script, not by the TSR.

To benefit from an engineered script, a caller needs skill in Controlled Phrasing to interrupt the typical pattern and Vocal Emphasis to make an embedded message effective.

Most telemarketing scripts sound alike when they are read. The length of the phrases are similar and familiar to both the TSR and the prospect:

> "*Good evening. How are you today?*"
> "*I am calling on behalf of ABC Company.*"
> "*May I speak to the owner?*"

Each of these opening lines end with a pause. The familiar words and phrases of the script, followed by a pause, create a *pattern*. We all learn to anticipate what follows next in the pattern. In most cases, it is a signal to hang up the phone.

Most communication depends on patterns. It helps make communication more efficient. We anticipate and react. You hold out your hand, I take it and shake it. You say, "*You know what?*" and I say, "*What?*". No one thinks about the response. We just do it: "*How are you today? Fine, how are you?*"

Unfortunately, patterns do not create rapport or build relationships. They are simply rituals. They take place without anyone being involved or even attentive.

If you *interrupt* a pattern, however, behaviors change drastically. People become alert, confused, and in need of closure. You offer me your hand in a greeting, but I just stand there and look at it. What happens next? No one knows. That interruption is the key to the beginning of your script.

If you can use your words and your voice to interrupt the familiar pattern of short phrase and quick hang-up, you greatly increase the chances of someone talking with you and giving you an invitation to continue the selling. Look at this sample opening script with marks (') added to indicate where it is safe to take a breath if needed:

> "*Hello. I'm Fred Brown, and MergerMania has asked me to* talk *to you' to help you see how you can save money on your phone bills. I only need to* talk *with you' about 3 minutes for you to decide if we can save you money. Is this a good time to talk to me?*"

The breath marks (') have been added to guide the TSR. These are suggestions for where a breath can be taken if necessary without creating a familiar pattern. Notice that none are at the ends of sentences. Breathing at the end of sentence is a familiar pattern. Interrupting that pattern requires a different breathing point. Adding breath marks to a script is helpful for callers.

By interrupting the pattern, the prospect is temporarily confused and open to suggestion. Consequently, when the final question is asked(*"Is this a good time..."*), the unconscious need for closure or resolution will lead to an inclination to say *"Yes."*

Controlled verbal phrasing is not easy. Because it goes against what feels "natural", it must be taught and practiced. But as one veteran caller once said to a newly hired TSR, "Quit complaining and try it. It really works!"

SKILL HINT:

A very easy pattern interrupt is to simply pause after you give your name:

"Hello. I'm Cyndi Harmon....."

Wait about two seconds before continuing. The prospect may acknowledge "Hello Cyndi" or may simply wait. Either way, you have created in the prospect a vacuum of curiosity that subconsciously invites you to talk more to fill the void and relieve the tension.

VOCAL EMPHASIS

Again, look at the sample script:

> *"Hello. I'm Fred Brown, and MergerMania has asked me to **talk** to you' to help you see how you can save*

*money on your phone bills. I only need to **talk** with you' about 3 minutes for you to decide if we can save you money. Is this a good time to **talk to me?**"*

The embedded commands are highlighted. But since the prospect cannot see this highlighting, the voice must create it. One approach would be to emphasize the word "talk". The motivational speaker knows how to emphasize a word when she commands, "**Seize** the moment, **Stand** up for your convictions, **Believe** in your strength". When Bill Clinton used statistics, he would say, "40...million...dollars..." to ensure that no one in the audience would mistakenly believe his numbers were insignificant. When Zig Ziglar says, "You need **Goals**", no one misses what he is talking about.

In the typical business application, however, such obvious emphasis is *not* effective in most cases, especially for selling on the phone. The trademark verbal accents of the motivational speaker are not the best technique for a TSR. Without the visual support of the speaker, such emphasis is too transparent and too aggressive for the phone.

The emphasis of an embedded command must be subtle. Subtle highlighting is the basis of what many call "subliminal messages." The embedded message must stand out but not in a noticeable way. The easiest way to highlight in a subtle fashion is to slow down your verbal pace for that one word (or pause a microsecond before and after), and drop the pitch slightly. With practice, you can deliver your message without anyone noticing the words that are being emphasized. The brain, however, will note the emphasis and react to the embedded message.

Practice reading the sample opening until you can maintain an upbeat and enthusiastic vocal style throughout while dropping your voice a bit and slowing your pace a little for the embedded words. And watch out for where you take a breath!

VOCAL PACING

Once you have advanced past the opening of your script, you will have an opportunity for dialogue with the prospect. You will hear how the prospect speaks and be able to match tone and speed. Such mirroring of vocal characteristics--or vocal pacing--increases rapport.

Vocal pacing also strengthens the TSRs' ability to establish and maintain rapport in non-scripted interactions. TSRs learn to listen and respond effectively. Often, a campaign may have several "mini-scripts", and the TSR can choose the script based on the prospects use of words (visual, auditory, or kinesthetic) or a particular interest revealed during conversation.

Vocal pacing requires rehearsal. Practice as many different tones and speeds as you can. Read a script or pretend you are having a discussion with someone. See how many different "voices" you can create. In a real telemarketing application, however, use only those "voices" with which you feel comfortable.

Be warned: if you do not practice, *all* voices different from yours will feel uncomfortable. This is not a good basis for judging. Practice, and then decide if there are some tones or speeds that make you uncomfortable.

You can also pace words and phrases. Repeat a phrase or word the prospect has used. It indicates you are listening and also helps you mirror that person. This is especially helpful with objections.

"I don't know. It makes me uncomfortable."
"Well, Ms. Brown, I don't want something to make you un- comfortable. Let's see if you will be more comfortable when you hear..." (KVA)

255

Finally, you can also pace language preference. Even if you do not know a person's overall language preference, matching the predicates during a key interaction will still help build rapport.

*"I don't **see** any value in this..."*
*"Let's **look** at two advantages for a moment..."*

*"I haven't **heard** anything any different from you..."*
*"Let me **tell** you about..."*

VOICEMAIL

Sometimes TSRs get frustrated by answering machines or voice-mail systems. Automatic dialers often make it impossible to leave messages with electronic systems. Yet, a good engineered script can make voice-mail or answering machines powerful selling tools. Since the prospect will probably listen to the message if it is well-written and well-delivered, it can be at least as effective as a live interaction!

A high-quality furniture manufacturer incorporated engineered messages into its telemarketing strategy. Shortly thereafter, they reported three results. First, they saw an immediate increase in responsiveness to their follow-up calls. (Sales could not be measured since they often were seeking bidding information and contract renewal data.) Second, when the messages were left on voice-mail, a marked increase in voluntary callbacks occurred. Third, when they called a second time, they were astonished by the number of people who responded, "Oh, yes, I remember your message on the phone."

Like any script, you must know what you want the prospect to do. In a live call, you want the prospect to talk to you. With a voice-mail message, however, the objective must be different.

In many cases, it is probably *"Call back"* or *"Look forward to our talking when I call back"*. The script needs an opening that:

1. **Emphasizes a personal relationship**
2. **Contains a VAK mix**
3. **Embeds the initial command message**

In addition, the caller needs to be expert at delivering the embedded message. Fortunately, voice-mail scripts can be rehearsed until they are perfect.

NOTE:

One trick with voice-mail messages is to position the phone number in the middle of the message. Since most scripts end with the number, the pattern is expected. Interrupting the pattern, as mentioned earlier, creates temporary mental confusion. If there is no pause after the number and the message simply continues, the prospect will probably be unable to recall the number. Therefore, the message will have to be replayed! Multiply your embedded messages by two, and you can begin to appreciate part of the power of a well-engineered voice-mail message.

EXERCISE

Vocal Flexibility

1. Read aloud the following paragraph in your "natural" manner.

> "Practice as many different tones and speeds as you can. Read a script or pretend you are having a discussion with someone. See how many different "voices" you can create. In a real telemarketing application, however, use only those "voices" with which you feel comfortable. Be warned, though: if you do not practice, *all* voices different from yours will feel uncomfortable. This is not a good basis for judging. Practice, and then decide if there are some tones or speeds that make you uncomfortable."

2. Now read it aloud... with a higher pitched voice.

3. ...with a lower voice.

4. ...with a faster speed.

5. ...with a much slower speed.

6. ...as if you were very bored.

7. ...as if you were so excited you could not wait to tell your best friend.

8. ...like Marlon Brando.

9. ...like Joan Rivers.

10. ...like Darth Vader.

Continue this exercise, seeking as many different "voices" as you can create. Be an actor and discover your own flexibility!

EXERCISE

Language Matching

Match the prospects language (predicate) preference:

1. That doesn't sound interesting to me.

2. I'm not sure. Maybe I should talk to my wife about this.

3. Can you send me something I can read on this?

4. I don't like buying over the phone.

5. You, ABC Co., RST Co., XYZ Co.--- your deals all look alike to me.

Sample answers:

1. *"Maybe when you* hear *about..." (A)*
2. *"Let's* talk *about what you can* tell *her..." (A)*
3. *"Sure, I can, but let me help you* see *the advantage of deciding today..." (V)*
4. *"A lot of people are* uncomfortable *with buying over the phone. Let me help you* feel *better when I* tell *you about the protection for you* built *into this offer..." (K, K, A, K)*
5. *"We won't* look *alike when I can help* show *you what to* look *for in the fine print!"(V)*

EXERCISE

Voice Mail

In the message below, identify the three key elements:

1. emphasizes a personal relationship
2. contains a VAK mix
3. embeds the initial command message(s)

"Hello. I am Alan Watkins. I am the Vice President of Lakin Associates. I am calling you to see if you want more information about "The Unfair Advantage," a training program on NLP techniques for business professionals. If you decide to call, I am Alan with Lakin Associates, and my number is 1-800-541-2818. We are a Chicago-based firm and will be in the Bay Area on August 27. I hope you or a representative will call me if you want to know more about The Unfair Advantage. If you decide to call, Lakin Associates will send a package to you immediately that explains the program. I look forward to our talking about August 27. Thank you."

Voice Mail Exercise: *Sample Answers*

"Hello. I am Alan Watkins. I am the Vice President of Lakin Associates. I am calling you to see if you want more information about "The Unfair Advantage," a training program on NLP techniques for business professionals. If you decide to call, I am Alan with Lakin Associates, and my number is 1-800-541-2818. We are a Chicago-based firm and will be in the Bay Area on August 27. I hope you or a representative will call me if you want to know more about The Unfair Advantage. If you decide to call, Lakin Associates will send a package to you immediately that explains the program. I look forward to our talking about August 27. Thank you."

Emphasize personal relationship:
"I am calling you..."
"My number..."
"Call me..."
"I look forward to our talking..."

VAK Mix:
See, want, call (V,K,A)

Embedded commands:
"Want more information"
"Decide to call" (2)
"Call.....want to know more"
"Look forward to our talking"

FYI: This voice-mail script was used to sell a training program for The Unfair Advantage. The calls were timed to ensure that no one answered the phone and the message could be left on an answering machine. 100% of those called responded by calling back! Unfortunately, many people do not listen to their own messages today, and we would not expect such a return. We would expect, however, to have an advantage that would yield a return rate greater than the standard for any given industry.

In the world of telemarketing, technology is often king. But technology is only the framework for the delivery of the message. If the message or the delivery are not well-engineered, the technology is wasted. When the script and the caller training are given careful attention, the results are easily seen. NLP and other psychological models can provide the basis for a well-designed script and training program. Selling and providing customer service over the phone is not easy. Selecting the right people, providing appropriate training, and developing well-engineered scripts can give you The Unfair TELEMARKETING Advantage.

For more ideas on using The Unfair Advantage in telemaketing, go to our website: www.SellWithNLP.com and click on the heading "The Unfair TELEMARKETING Advantage". In that section, we tell about the new online lessons to help you enjoy the power of an engineered telemarketing message.

Enjoy The Unfair Advantage!

SELL WITH NLP!

ADDENDUM

The Unfair Advantage Checklist A-2

NLP Language Preference Indicator© .. A-5

Live Workshop Outline A-12

The On-Demand Online Lessons A-14

Checklist of The Unfair Advantage Techniques

SALES CALL AND PROSPECT INTERVIEWING

Did you avoid the "Golden Rule"?
Did you make sure you had an "invitation"?
Did you identify your prospect's desired outcome?

Did you begin with non-verbal mirroring (pacing)?
Did you continue to mirror non-verbally?
Did you "test" rapport by breaking your non-verbal pacing?

Did you note VAK preference early on?
Did you phrase initial questions using VAK preference?
Did you ask key questions with all three VAK styles?

Did you notice eye movement in moments of silence?
Did you notice eye movement after key questions?
Did you use eye movement to guide your next question?
Did you ask question quickly after noticing eye movement?

Did you use embedded messages at each phase of the call?
Did you use stories, metaphors, or jokes to send a message?
Did you include enough Digital or technical jargon for credibility?

Did you probe for the VAK buying strategy?
Did you notice the eyes as well as the words?
Did you phrase your comments using the VAK strategy?

Did you use your business card or brochure to keep the advantage?
Did you explore future behaviors to keep the advantage?

LETTERS

Did you open with VAK balance?
Did you close with VAK balance?
Did you avoid Digital words?
Did you embed key message at least three times?
Did you close with an embedded command?

FORMAL PRESENTATIONS/ TEAM SELLING

Did you non-verbally mirror the key people prior to your presentation?
Did your partner mirror key people?
Did you achieve mirroring with the whole group?
Did you mirror anyone asking a question?
Did you mirror with eye contact?

Did you mix VAK language?
Did you have a VAK mix for overall presentation (handouts, overheads, discussion areas, etc.)?
Did your partner cue you to repeat a key phrase using a different VAK preference?

Did you use handouts to keep the advantage?
Did you avoid competing with the content?

TELEMARKETING

Did you pace the voice of the other person?
Did you identify your desired action?
Did you prepare a script with embedded action commands?
Did your script have a rich VAK mix?
Did you emphasize a personal relationship with the script?
Did you use short words?
Did you recognize where hang-ups occurred and add new script elements?

Did you deliver your script with energy?

Did you present your script in a way to avoid familiar patterns?

Did you leave messages with embedded messages?

Did you leave messages with an interruption to the familiar patterns?

LANGUAGE PREFERENCE INDICATOR (LPI)©

Circle the answer that fits you best:

1. When I attend a seminar or a class, I benefit most when I:
   a. have notes and handouts to read and follow-along.
   b. listen intently to a good speaker.
   c. can engage in activities or role-playing

2. Which is most like you?
   a. I can remember what a person's voice sounds like after I have met him/her.
   b. I often feel good or bad about someone without having any specific reason.
   c. I need to see someone to be comfortable with that person.

3. When I have a lot of things to do, I am most comfortable when I can:
   a. begin with a written to-do list to guide me.
   b. talk to others about what needs to be done.
   c. just get started and attack one thing at a time.

4. When I encounter a problem with a task, I prefer to:
   a. ask someone or talk to myself as I go through the options.
   b. trust my instincts and try something.
   c. visualize it over and over until I can see how to solve it.

5. I think an audience prefers speakers who:
   a. use slides and overheads .
   b. act as facilitators and generate discussions.
   c. conduct demonstrations and give people a hands-on experience.

6. Which is most like you?
   a. I would rather do an oral exercise than a written one.
   b. I trust my "gut reaction" on test questions (and am not likely to re-read a test).
   c. I would rather see something in writing or illustration than have it explained to me.

7. If you were to lose one of the following,, which would be most upsetting to you?
   a. your vision
   b. your hearing
   c. your ability to move your arms or legs

8. When I try to remember someone I just met, I:
   a. associate the sound of his/her name to something else.
   b. concentrate on getting a sense of who the person is and what makes him/her tick.
   c. picture their name written on a name tag or paper.

9. I learn most about a person by:
   a. looking at him/her, especially the face.
   b. listening to words and voice tone
   c. noticing attitude or posture

10. If someone is explaining something important to me, I:
    a. may look away while concentrating on their words or whatI need to remember or say back

    b. lower my head and listen intently, as if trying to absorb what they are saying

    c. am likely to look directly at them or close my eyes to avoid being distracted while trying to see their point.

11. Think about a friend from your high school days; which experience lingers?:
    a. a picture of the person in your mind
    b. the sound of the person's voice
    c. your feelings about that person

12. When participating in a problem-solving group, I like to:
    a. discuss everyone's ideas.
    b. find the approach that feels right and explore that one in more depth.
    c. have several options to look at.

13. I consider myself to be a:
    a. visual person, able to quickly visualize an idea
    b. auditory person, able to listen and learn from what I hear
    c. kinesthetic or feeling person, quick to get a gut-feeling for something.

14. When I am experiencing a high degree of tension, I am most likely to:
    a. talk to myself, maybe outloud at times, to guide my actions.
    b. just want to make something happen; can't stand inaction.
    c. visualize the problem solved and then begin to act or make a list.

15. My typical speaking voice is probably described by others as:
    a. quick, sometimes high pitched.
    b. having an even or rhythmic tempo; range is midway between high and low.
    c. slow and maybe deep or low; often with long pauses; maybe sometimes breathy.

16. When I am under pressure, my breathing is typically:
    a. even, from the whole chest, sometimes with prolonged exhaling.
    b. deep and full, low in the stomach.
    c. high and shallow; sometimes I even skip a breath.

17. When I want to make a good impression on someone I have not met, I prefer to:
    a. write a letter.
    b. talk on the phone.
    c. meet during a meeting or while I am engaging in another activity, like a class or a sport.

18. The following best describes me on "bad days":
    a. an internal voice often nags me.
    b. frequently feel uneasy without knowing why.
    c. see myself in a negative way.

19. I am most likely to trust:
    a. what I see
    b. what I hear
    c. what I feel

20. On vacation, I prefer to :
    a. meet and talk to people; or discuss the days' activities each evening.

b. do as many things as I can fit in the schedule.

c. enjoy photographs of the vacation and the things I saw.

21. When I go to a movie, I get most upset if:

    a. the picture is out of focus or the frame is uneven (with part of the top of the picture showing at the bottom).

    b. the sound is fuzzy or if there is a hiss

    c. the soundtrack is too loud

22. If I need to send a note or letter, I:

    a. could dictate my note with little need to edit or check it.

    b. may pace and dictate or think while I walk about.

    c. like to see my ideas on paper much as they may appear in the final draft before I am comfortable.

To find out what your Preferred Language may be, score your answers on the following page.

Scoring your test:

For items 1,3,5,7,9,11,13,15,17,19, & 21, count and record the number of times you circled the following choices:

TABLE ONE

(V)	(A)	(K)
Choice a =	Choice b =	Choice c =

For items 2,4,6,8,10,12,14,16,18, 20 & 22:

TABLE TWO

(A)	(K)	(V)
Choice a =	Choice b =	Choice c =

Now add the scores as follows:

Table One "a" score plus Table Two "c" score = _____
(Visual Language Preference)

Table One "b" score plus Table Two "a" score = _____
(Auditory Language Preference)

Table One "c" score plus Table Two "b" score = _____
(Kinesthetic Language Preference)

NOTE: This is only an experimental test. It may give you a hint of your preference in your day-to-day use of language. For most of your use of language, expect to use a mix of language preferences. But under stress or with certain topics, you are likely to show a marked preference. Begin to notice your preferred words as well as those used by others. And remember, no language is any better than another. Only different.

The Unfair Advantage® Workshop
SELL WITH NLP!

1. Introduction to the Selling Process and NLP as a powerful set of listening and communication tools to help control the selling process by emphasizing *rapport* and *mental rehearsal.*

   (How to sell YOU!)

2. Language Pacing for Rapport

   (Learn to speak your prospect's language and "pace" Visual, Auditory, and Kinesthetic language.)

3. Language Mixing for Impact

   (Practice mixing language preferences to increase the visual, auditory, and kinesthetic "arousal" state of your audience.)

4. Eye Cues

   (Discover how to read eyes to identify language preference, rapport level, and buying strategies.)

5. Non-Language Pacing

   (Practice non-verbal pacing; also learn to pace vocal characteristics. Includes ideas for pacing in team and group presentations.)

6. Precision Probing

   (Learn how to ask the key questions that will clarify what a client means.)

7. Mindsets (Metaprograms)

(Learn to use phrases that match a client's view of the world.)

8. Leading with Action Commands
(Discover skills for delivering suggestions that lead to actions.)

9. Embedding Commands

(See how to "hide" a command and make it virtually subliminal; enabling the mind to rehearse the action you desire without inviting resistance. Examples include how to write scripts for phone campaigns, presentations or direct-mail copy.)

10. Handling Objections without Losing Rapport

(Learn three simple skills for reducing hostility and getting past objections.)

11. Keeping the Advantage

(How to help the client or prospect keep YOU in their mind.)

12. Putting it Together

(Opportunity to write a letter, construct a telesales script, plan a sales call or presentation, or write brochure copy that uses many of the above skills. Get guidance and feedback from Dr. Lakin and from other participants.)

Want to know more?

In-depth online Lessons,
YOUR schedule, YOUR pace
www.sellwithnlp.com
(Descriptions on next pages)

Do you need the ten on-demand online lessons of *The Unfair Advantage?*

Look at these questions and ask yourself.

1. **There are languages hidden beneath the words you speak. Do you know what they look or sound like? Do you know how to use them to be more effective?** (Want an advantage?...Lesson One: *"Introduction to the Brain"*...<u>FREE</u>)

   What you will learn in Lesson One:
   1. How someone's brain filters what YOU say.
   2. How someone's words can tell you what filter someone is using
   3. The importance of "engineering" your message to get past filters
   4. The difference between Visual, Auditory, and Kinesthetic words and why you should care
   5. The risk of Digital words that are the common "business" vocabulary
   6. The outlines for the other nine workshops

2. **You need to write a letter to get an appointment with a prospect. Do you know what to say to get results?** (Want an advantage?...Lesson Two: *"Scripts to get Invited"*)

   What you will learn in Lesson Two:
   1. How to describe your value in writing
   2. How to energize your message with a "VAK mix"

3. How to include an Action Command in your script
4. The SIX key elements in a written note or script to differentiate yourself
   a. Make it Personal
   b. Implied Reason for the meeting
   c. "Relationship Bridge"
   d. Present benefits with a VAK mix
   e. Action Command
   f. Make a Contract
5. The SEVEN elements of a follow-up script
6. How to write Callback Scripts and "Call-Request" Scripts
7. How to appeal to the gatekeeper
8. Special tips for using e-mails to get invited
9. Special tips for using letters to get invited

3. **You see you have a meeting scheduled with a key prospect or customer. Do you know how to prepare (what to say, how to say it, etc.) so that your time with the prospect is well used?** (Want an advantage?...Lesson Three: *"Warm the Cold Call"*)

What you will learn in Lesson Three:
1. How to avoid the "Buyer/Seller Dance"
2. How to choose a real Action Command for the first meeting
3. How to benefit from you already know (and how to know you need more information)
4. How to focus your early comments on Benefits to the customer
5. How to plan your opening statement
   a. Confirming your contract

b. Opening BENEFIT/VALUE statement with VAK Mix

c. Compelling question to engage the prospect

6. How to check your own attitude about "cold calls"

4. **You are about to see a new prospect. Do you know what to say and do in the first two minutes to gain rapport, present yourself, and keep a contract with the prospect?** (Want an advantage?...Lesson Four: *"Sell YOU at the First Meeting"*)

What you will learn in Lesson Four:
1. How to confirm the contract
2. How to build trust immediately with Physical Mirroring
3. How to mirror a group
4. How to use mirroring to recover lost rapport
5. How to "echo mirror" to hold rapport

5. **You want to be a consultative seller. Do you know how to ask questions to see what the prospect or customer really needs and wants?** (Want an advantage?...Lesson Five: *"Learn What the Customer Really Wants"*)

What you will learn in Lesson Five:
1. The reality that there are only perceptions and the need to learn what the customer sees
2. How to avoid the "Question Traps" that have hidden assumptions
3. The power of being "present", especially when combined with mirroring

4. How to listen actively
5. The power of being curious
6. How to avoid "Mind Reading"
7. The six questions to prevent "Mind Reading" and to help you understand the customer

6. **You want your prospect or customer thinking about the outcome YOU want to see occur without creating resistance. Do you know what to say to do that?** (Want an advantage?...Lesson Six: *"Lead the Process with Embedded Action Commands"*)

What you will learn in Lesson Six:
1. Selling is more than building trust
2. How to use Action Commands to lead the process
3. How to embed an action command to avoid resistance
4. Six ways to embed a command
    a. With a negative
    b. With the "three B's"
    c. In a quote
    d. With redirection
    e. With a question
5. When no one is noticing

7. **Your customer or prospect has a fairly rigid way of looking at the world. Do you know how to say your ideas or suggestions to fit that view and reduce resistance?** (Want an advantage? Lesson Seven: *"Customerize the Proposal to Fit Prospect's Mind"*)

What you will learn in Lesson Seven:
1. Every person's view of the world is unique
2. How to avoid assuming you know what the customer wants
3. How to learn how your customer views the world
4. How to adapt your proposals to fit that world view or "Mindset (metaprogram)"
5. The six most useful Mindsets and how to use them in sales

8. **Your customer or prospect raises a tough objection. Do you know what to say first and how to respond to keep rapport?** (Want an advantage? Lesson Eight: *"Handle Objections without Losing Trust/Rapport"*)

What you will learn in Lesson Eight:
1. That objections can either give you insights or cost you money
2. The source of most objections
3. How to be present and seek understanding
4. How to Pace-Link-and Lead to redirect the focus and lead the process
5. How to "Reframe" and "Future Pace" to prevent new objections
6. How to use the "VAK Invisible Handshake" to reduce resistance

9. **You want to be in the best possible frame of mind to sell, because your attitude and expectations can determine an outcome. Do you know how to be more successful by changing what you say to yourself and how you look**

at the future? (Want an advantage? Lesson Nine: *"Fine-Tune Your Own Attitude"*)

What you will learn in Lesson Nine:
1. Many sales are lost before you even contact the prospect
2. Your brain listens to what you say to yourself
3. If you think you can or cannot, you are right
4. The difference between "empowering" and "limiting" beliefs
5. The dangerous words you say to yourself
6. How to discover your own limiting beliefs
7. How to overcome you limiting beliefs
8. How to become an optimist
9. How to energize yourself with your own goals

10. **You have to sell (close) or upsell in one phone call. Do you know how to script what you want to say and deliver that message so you will see the results you want?** (Want an advantage? Lesson Ten: *"Telemarketing Scripting for Inbound/Outbound One-Call Selling"*)

What you will learn in Lesson Ten:
1. You have 3-5 seconds to sell yourself and become a person over the phone
2. You have only two tools: Your scripts and your voice
3. How to decide how to use the EIGHT possible script elements
4. The importance of a script designed to get an action
5. How to use mini-scripts
6. Key scripting tools
   a. Pattern interrupt

     b. Relationship Bridge

     c. Implied Reason

     d. "You" and "me"

7. The power of the "opening trance"
8. How to write an "engage script" to use when the prospect begins to talk with you
9. How to write an "offer script" with commands to get a action
10. How to deliver your words effectively
11. The importance of being able to have a conversation
12. How to check your own attitude and expectations

THE UNFAIR ADVANTAGE

SELL WITH NLP!

Made in the USA
Lexington, KY
20 October 2016